READING IN THE CONTENT AREAS
LITERATURE 1

Laura Stark Johnson

PERMISSIONS

ALFRED A. KNOPF, INC. for "Harlem." From *Collected Poems* by Langston Hughes. Copyright 1951 by Langston Hughes. Reprinted by permission of Alfred A. Knopf, Inc.

DIAL BOOKS FOR YOUNG READERS for excerpt from *Roll of Thunder, Hear My Cry* by Mildred D. Taylor. Text copyright © 1976 by Mildred D. Taylor. Reprinted by permission of the publisher, Dial Books for Young Readers.

DOUBLEDAY, A DIVISION OF BANTAM, DOUBLEDAY, DELL PUBLISHING GROUP, INC. for "My Marshmallow Fudge Wonder Diet" by Jean Kerr. From *How I Got to Be Perfect*. Copyright © 1978 by Collins Productions, Inc. Reprinted by permission of Doubleday, a division of Bantam, Doubleday, Dell Publishing Group.

THE ESTATE OF QUENTIN REYNOLDS for "A Secret for Two" by Quentin Reynolds. Copyright 1936, Crowell-Collier Publishing Co. Reprinted by permission of the Estate of Quentin Reynolds.

THE ESTATE OF THE LATE SONIA BROWNELL ORWELL AND MARTIN SECKER AND WARBURG LTD. for excerpt from *Animal Farm* by George Orwell. Copyright © The estate of the late Sonia Brownell Orwell and Martin Secker and Warburg Ltd.

HARCOURT BRACE & COMPANY for excerpt from *Animal Farm* by George Orwell, copyright 1946 by Harcourt Brace & Company, renewed 1974 by Sonia Orwell, reprinted by permission of the publisher.

for excerpt from *The People, Yes* by Carl Sandburg, copyright 1936 by Harcourt Brace & Company, renewed 1964 by Carl Sandburg, reprinted by permission of the publisher.

for excerpt from *I Remember Mama,* copyright 1945 by John Van Druten, renewed 1973 by Carter Lodge, Executor of the Estate of John Van Druten, reprinted by permission of Harcourt Brace & Company.

HENRY HOLT AND COMPANY, INC. for "Stopping by Woods on a Snowy Evening" by Robert Frost. Copyright 1923 by Holt, Rinehart and Winston and renewed 1951 by Robert Frost. Reprinted from *The Poetry of Robert Frost* edited by Edward Connery Lathem, by permission of Henry Holt and Company, Inc.

HOUGHTON MIFFLIN COMPANY for excerpt from *Farewell to Manzanar* by Jeanne Wakatsuki and James D. Houston. Copyright © 1973 by James D. Houston. Reprinted by permission of Houghton Mifflin Company.

THE PUBLISHERS AND THE TRUSTEES OF AMHERST COLLEGE for "A Bird came down the Walk" by Emily Dickinson. Reprinted by permission of the publishers and the Trustees of Amherst College from *The Poems of Emily Dickinson,* edited by Thomas H. Johnson, Cambridge, Mass.: The Belknap Press of Harvard University Press, Copyright 1951, © 1955, 1979, 1983 by The President and Fellows of Harvard College.

RANDOM HOUSE, INC. for excerpt from *Out of Africa* by Isak Dinesen. Copyright 1937 by Random House, Inc. and renewed 1965 by Rungstedlundfonden. Reprinted by permission of the publisher.

for excerpt from *A Raisin in the Sun* by Lorraine Hansberry. Copyright © 1958 by Robert Nemiroff, as an unpublished work. Copyright © 1959, 1966, 1984 by Robert Nemiroff. Reprinted by permission of Random House, Inc.

CAUTION: Professionals and amateurs are hereby warned that *A Raisin in the Sun,* being fully protected under the Copyright Laws of the United States of America, the British Empire, including the Dominion of Canada, and all other countries of the Universal Copyright and Berne Conventions, is subject to royalty. All rights, including professional, amateur, motion picture, recitation, lecturing, public reading, radio and television broadcasting, and the rights of translation into foreign languages, are strictly reserved. Particular emphasis is laid on the question of readings, permission for which must be secured in writing. All inquiries should be addressed to the publisher.

HELEN AND ROSEMARY A. THURBER for "The Secret Life of Walter Mitty" by James Thurber. Copyright © 1942 James Thurber. Copyright © 1970 Helen Thurber and Rosemary A. Thurber. From *My World—and Welcome To It,* published by Harcourt Brace Jovanovich, Inc.

TV GUIDE® MAGAZINE for "Daytime Soaps: The Best and the Brightest" by Molly Ivins. Reprinted with permission from TV Guide® Magazine. Copyright © 1988 by Triangle Publications, Inc. Radnor, Pennsylvania.

Reading in the Content Areas, Literature 1
ISBN 978-0-88336-109-2

Copyright © 1990 New Readers Press
New Readers Press
A Publishing Division of ProLiteracy
1320 Jamesville Avenue, Syracuse, New York 13210
www.newreaderspress.com

Printed in the United States of America
19   18   17   16   15

All proceeds from the sale of New Readers Press materials support literacy programs in the United States and worldwide.

Project Editor: Christina M. Jagger
Manuscript Editor: Margaret Duckett
Cover Design: Patricia Rapple
Cover Illustration: Stephen Rhodes
Composition: Anne Hyde

Table of Contents

Unit 1: Short Stories

I can't write without a reader.
It's precisely like a kiss—you can't do it alone.
John Cheever

As you read the short stories in this unit, you will read about times past and present and about places far and near. You will meet a number of characters. You may discover that some of these characters have thoughts, feelings, or experiences similar to your own. Other characters may think and act in ways you wouldn't even consider.

As you read each story, get involved in it. Pretend that you are there—on the scene, observing everything that happens. Picture the time and place, the characters, and the events as they unfold. Bring your own experiences to the story. Compare how you are feeling with the character's reactions. Don't be afraid to laugh or to feel sad or angry.

Think about each story when you have finished reading it. Did you enjoy it? Could you relate to it? Did you learn something about human nature so that you understand yourself or others a little better?

Have a good time reading these short stories and sharing your reactions with your classmates.

*What do you do when you want to get away from it all?
In this short story, Rip Van Winkle would often take his
dog and go hunting to escape life's pressures. What
happened to Rip one particular time has entertained
people for more than 170 years. As you read, picture
Rip's life before that time and when he returns 20 years
later!*

Rip Van Winkle

Washington Irving (1783–1859)

Whoever has made a voyage up the Hudson must remember the Kaatskill Mountains. They are a branch of the great Appalachian family, and are seen away to the west of the river, swelling up to a noble height, and lording it over the surrounding country. Every change of season, every change of weather, indeed, every hour of the day produces some change in the magical hues[1] and shapes of these mountains.

At the foot of these fairy mountains, the voyager may have descried[2] the light smoke curling up from a village. It is a little village of great antiquity, having been founded by some of the Dutch colonists in the early time of the province, just about the beginning of the government of the good Peter Stuyvesant[3] (may he rest in peace!) and there were some of the houses of the original settlers standing within a few years, built of small yellow bricks brought from Holland. In that same village, and in one of these very houses (which, to tell the precise truth, was sadly time-worn and weather-beaten) there lived, many years since, while the country was yet a province of

---

1. **hues:** colors.
2. **descried:** discovered.
3. **Peter Stuyvesant:** the Dutch governor of the Colony of New Amsterdam from 1646 to 1664.

Great Britain, a simple, good-natured fellow, of the name of Rip Van Winkle.

He was a great favorite among all the good wives of the village, who, as usual with the amiable sex, took his part in all family squabbles, and never failed, whenever they talked those matters over in their evening gossipings, to lay all the blame on Dame Van Winkle. The children of the village, too, would shout with joy whenever he approached. He assisted at their sports, made their playthings, taught them to fly kites and shoot marbles, and told them long stories of ghosts, witches, and Indians. Whenever he went dodging about the village, he was surrounded by a troop of them clambering on his back and playing a thousand tricks on him with impunity;[4] and not a dog would bark at him throughout the neighborhood.

The great error in Rip's composition was an insuperable aversion[5] to all kinds of profitable labor. It could not be from the want of assiduity or perseverance;[6] for he would sit on a wet rock and fish all day without a murmur, even though he should not be encouraged by a single nibble. He would carry a fowling-piece[7] on his shoulder for hours together, trudging through woods and swamps, and up hill and down dale, to shoot a few squirrels or wild pigeons. He would never refuse to assist a neighbor even in the roughest toil, and was a foremost man at all county frolics for husking Indian corn, or building stone fences; the women of the village, too, used to employ him to run their errands, and to do such little odd jobs as their less obliging husbands would not do for them. In a word, Rip was ready to attend to anybody's business but his own; but as to doing family duty and keeping his farm in order, he found it impossible.

His children, too, were as ragged and wild as if they belonged to nobody. His son Rip, an urchin begotten in his own likeness, promised to inherit the habits, with the old clothes, of his father.

Rip Van Winkle, however, was one of those happy mortals, of foolish, well-oiled dispositions, who take the world easy, eat white bread or brown, whichever can be got with least thought or trouble, and would rather starve on a penny than work for a pound. If left to himself, he would have whistled life away, in perfect contentment; but his wife kept continually dinning in his ears about his idleness, his carelessness, and the ruin he was bringing on his family. Morning, noon, and night, her tongue was incessantly going, and everything he said or did was sure to produce a torrent of household eloquence.

Rip's sole domestic adherent was his dog Wolf, who was as much henpecked as his master; for Dame Van Winkle regarded them as companions in idleness, and even looked upon Wolf with an evil eye as the cause of his master's going so often astray. Times

---

4. impunity: no punishment.
5. insuperable aversion: overwhelming dislike.
6. assiduity or perseverance: patience or persistence.
7. fowling piece: shotgun.

grew worse and worse with Rip Van Winkle as years of matrimony rolled on.

Poor Rip was at last reduced almost to despair; and his only alternative, to escape from the labor of the farm and the clamor of his wife, was to take a gun in hand, and stroll away into the woods. Here he would sometimes seat himself at the foot of a tree, and share the contents of his wallet with Wolf, with whom he sympathized as a fellow-sufferer in persecution.

In a long ramble of the kind, on a fine autumnal day, Rip had unconsciously scrambled to one of the highest parts of the Kaatskill Mountains. He was after his favorite sport of squirrel-shooting, and the still solitudes had echoed and re-echoed with the reports of his gun. Panting and fatigued, he threw himself, late in the afternoon, on a green knoll, covered with mountain herbage, that crowned the brow of the precipice.

For some time Rip lay musing on this scene; evening was gradually advancing; the mountains began to throw their long blue shadows over the valleys; he saw that it would be dark long before he could reach the village; and he heaved a heavy sigh when he thought of encountering the terrors of Dame Van Winkle.

As he was about to descend, he heard a voice from a distance hallooing: "Rip Van Winkle! Rip Van Winkle!" He looked around, but could see nothing but a crow winging its solitary flight across the mountain. He thought his fancy must have deceived him, and turned again to descend, when he heard the same cry ring through the still, evening air, "Rip Van Winkle! Rip Van Winkle!"—at the same time Wolf bristled up his back, and giving a low growl, skulked to his master's side, looking fearfully down into the glen. Rip now felt a vague apprehension[8] stealing over him; he looked anxiously in the same direction, and perceived a strange figure slowly toiling up the rocks, and bending under the weight of something he carried on his back. He was surprised to see any human being in this lonely and unfrequented place, but supposing it to be someone of the neighborhood in need of his assistance, he hastened down to yield it.

On nearer approach, he was still more surprised at the stranger's appearance. He was a short, square-built old fellow, with thick bushy hair, and a grizzled beard. His dress was of the antique Dutch fashion—a cloth jerkin[9] strapped round the waist—several pairs of breeches, the outer one decorated with rows of buttons down the sides, and bunches at the knees. He bore on his shoulders a stout keg, that seemed full of liquor, and made signs for Rip to approach and assist him with the load. Though rather shy and distrustful of this new acquaintance, Rip complied; and they clambered up a narrow gully. As they ascended, Rip every now and then heard long rolling

---

8. **apprehension:** fear.
9. **jerkin:** sleeveless jacket.

Detail from SCENE ON THE HUDSON (RIP VAN WINKLE), 1845, James Hamilton. National Museum of American Art, Smithsonian Institution, Museum purchase

peals, like distant thunder, that seemed to issue out of a deep ravine, or rather cleft between lofty rocks, toward which their rugged path conducted. He paused for an instant, but supposing it to be the muttering of one of those transient thundershowers which often take place in the mountain heights, he proceeded. Passing through the ravine, they came to a hollow, like a small amphitheatre.

On entering the amphitheatre, new objects of wonder presented themselves. On a level spot in the center was a company of odd-looking personages playing at ninepins.[10] They were dressed in quaint outlandish fashion; some wore short doublets, others jerkins, with long knives in their belts, and most of them had enormous breeches, of similar style with that of the guide's. They all had beards of various shapes and colors. There was one who seemed to be the commander. He was a stout old gentleman, with a weather-beaten countenance; he wore a laced doublet, broad belt and hanger, high-crowned hat and feather, red stockings, and high-heeled shoes with roses on them. As Rip and his companion approached them they suddenly desisted from their play, and stared at him with such fixed statue-like gaze, that his heart turned within him, and his knees smote together. His companion now emptied the contents of the keg into large flagons,[11] and made signs to him to wait upon the

10. **ninepins:** a type of bowling.
11. **flagons:** bottles.

company. He obeyed with fear and trembling; they quaffed the liquor in profound silence, and then returned to their game.

By degrees, Rip's awe and apprehension subsided. He even ventured, when no eye was fixed upon him, to taste the beverage, which he found had much of the flavor of excellent Hollands.[12] He was naturally a thirsty soul, and was soon tempted to repeat the draught. One taste provoked another; and he reiterated his visits to the flagon so often, that at length his senses were overpowered, his eyes swam in his head, his head gradually declined, and he fell into a deep sleep.

On waking, he found himself on the green knoll whence he had first seen the old man of the glen. He rubbed his eyes—it was a bright, sunny morning. "Surely," thought Rip, "I have not slept here all night." He recalled the occurrences before he fell asleep. The strange man with the keg of liquor— the mountain ravine—the wild retreat among the rocks—the woebegone party at ninepins—the flagon—"Oh, that flagon! That wicked flagon!" thought Rip—"What excuse shall I make to Dame Van Winkle?"

He looked round for his gun, but in place of the clean well-oiled fowling-piece, he found an old firelock lying by him, the barrel incrusted with rust, the lock falling off, and the stock worm-eaten. He now suspected that the grave roysterers of the mountain had put a trick upon him, and having dosed him with liquor, had robbed him of his gun. Wolf, too, had disappeared, but he might have strayed away after a squirrel or partridge. He whistled after him and shouted his name, but all in vain; no dog was to be seen.

He determined to revisit the scene of the last evening's gambol, and if he met with any of the party, to demand his dog and gun. As he rose to walk, he found himself stiff in the joints. "These mountain beds do not agree with me," thought Rip, "and if this frolic should lay me up with a fit of rheumatism, I shall have a blessed time with Dame Van Winkle." With some difficulty he got down into the glen; he found the gully up which he and his companion had ascended the preceding evening; but to his astonishment a mountain stream was now foaming down it.

Here, then, poor Rip was brought to a stand. He again called and whistled after his dog; he was only answered by the cawing of a flock of idle crows, sporting high in the air. What was to be done? The morning was passing away, and Rip felt famished for want of his breakfast. He grieved to give up his dog and gun; he dreaded to meet his wife; but it would not do to starve among the mountains. He shook his head, shouldered the rusty firelock, and, with a heart full of trouble and anxiety, turned his steps homeward.

As he approached the village, he met a number of people, but none whom he knew, which somewhat surprised him, for he had thought himself acquainted with everyone in the country round. Their dress, too,

---

12. **Hollands:** Dutch gin.

THE RETURN OF RIP VAN WINKLE; John Quidor; National Gallery of Art, Washington; Andrew W. Mellon Collection

was of a different fashion from that to which he was accustomed. They all stared at him with equal marks of surprise, and whenever they cast their eyes upon him, invariably stroked their chins. The constant recurrence of this gesture induced Rip, involuntarily, to do the same, when, to his astonishment, he found his beard had grown a foot long!

He had now entered the skirts of the village. A troop of strange children ran at his heels, hooting after him, and pointing at his gray beard. The dogs, too, not one of which he recognized, barked at him as he passed. The very village was altered: it was larger and more populous. There were rows of houses which he had never seen before, and those which had been his familiar haunts had disappeared. Strange names were over the doors—strange faces at the windows—everything was strange. He began to doubt whether both he and the world around him were not bewitched. Surely this was his native village, which he had left but the day before. There stood the Kaatskill Mountains—there ran the silver Hudson at a distance—there was every hill and dale precisely as it had always been—Rip was sorely perplexed— "That flagon last night," thought he, "has addled my poor head sadly!"

It was with some difficulty that he found the way to his own house, which he approached with silent awe, expecting every moment to hear the shrill voice of Dame Van Winkle. He found the house gone to decay—the roof fallen in, the windows shattered, and the doors off the hinges. A half-starved dog, that looked like Wolf, was skulking about it. Rip called him by name, but the cur snarled, showed his teeth, and passed on. This was an unkind cut indeed. "My very dog," sighed poor Rip, "has forgotten me!"

He entered the house, which, to tell the truth, Dame Van Winkle had always kept in neat order. It was empty, forlorn, and apparently abandoned. He called loudly for his wife and children—the lonely chambers rang for a moment with his voice, and then all again was silence. He now hurried forth, and hastened to his old resort, the village inn—but it, too, was gone. A large rickety wooden building stood in its place, and over the door was painted, "The Union Hotel, by Jonathan Doolittle." Instead of the great tree that used to shelter the quiet little Dutch inn of yore, there now was reared a tall naked pole, with something on the top that looked like a red nightcap, and from it was fluttering a flag, on which was a singular assemblage of stars and stripes—all this was strange and incomprehensible. He recognized on the sign, however, the ruby face of King George, under which he had smoked so many a peaceful pipe, but even this was singularly metamorphosed.[13] The red coat was changed for one of blue and buff, a sword was held in the hand instead of a sceptre, the head was decorated with a cocked hat, and underneath was painted in large characters, "GENERAL WASHINGTON."

There was, as usual, a crowd of folk about the door, but none that Rip remembered. The very character of the people seemed changed. There was a busy, bustling tone about it, instead of the accustomed phlegm and drowsy tranquility.

The appearance of Rip, with his long, grizzled beard, his rusty fowling-piece, his uncouth dress, and an army of women and children at his heels, soon attracted the attention of the tavern politicians. They crowded round him, eyeing him from head to foot with great curiosity. Rip stared in vacant stupidity. A short but busy little fellow pulled him by the arm, and rising on tiptoe, inquired in his ear, "whether he was Federal or Democrat."[14] Rip was at a loss to comprehend the question; when a knowing, self-important old gentleman in a sharp cocked hat, made his way through the crowd, and planting himself before Van Winkle, demanded, "What brought him to the election with a gun on his shoulder, and a mob at his heels; and whether he meant to breed a riot in the village?"

"Alas, gentlemen!" cried Rip, somewhat dismayed, "I am a poor, quiet man, a native of this place, and a

13. metamorphosed: changed.
14. Federal or Democrat: two political parties.

loyal subject of the King, God bless him!"

Here a general shout burst from the bystanders—"A tory![15] A tory! A spy! A refugee! Hustle him! Away with him!" It was with great difficulty that the self-important man in the cocked hat restored order and demanded again of the unknown culprit what he came there for, and whom he was seeking. The poor man humbly assured him that he meant no harm, but merely came there in search of some of his neighbors, who used to keep about the tavern.

"Well—who are they? Name them."

Rip bethought himself a moment, and inquired, "Where's Nicholas Vedder?"

There was a silence for a little while, when an old man replied, in a thin, piping voice, "Nicholas Vedder? Why, he is dead and gone these eighteen years. There was a wooden tombstone in the churchyard that used to tell all about him, but that's rotten and gone, too."

"Where's Brom Dutcher?"

"Oh, he went off to the army in the beginning of the war; some say he was killed at the storming of Stony Point— others say he was drowned in a squall at the foot of Antony's Nose. I don't know—he never came back again."

"Where's Van Brummel, the schoolmaster?"

"He went off to the wars, too; was a great militia general, and is now in Congress."

Rip's heart died away, at hearing of these sad changes in his home and friends, and finding himself thus alone in the world. Every answer puzzled him, too, by treating of such enormous lapses of time, and of matters which he could not understand: war—Congress— Stony Point;—he had no courage to ask after any more friends, but cried out in despair, "Does nobody here know Rip Van Winkle?"

"Oh, Rip Van Winkle!" exclaimed two or three. "Oh, to be sure! that's Rip Van Winkle yonder, leaning against the tree."

Rip looked, and beheld a precise counterpart of himself as he went up the mountain; apparently as lazy, and certainly as ragged. The poor fellow was now completely confounded. He doubted his own identity, and whether he was himself or another man. In the midst of his bewilderment, the man in the cocked hat demanded who he was and what was his name?

"God knows!" exclaimed he at his wit's end; "I'm not myself—I'm somebody else—that's me yonder—no— that's somebody else, got into my shoes—I was myself last night, but I fell asleep on the mountain, and they've changed my gun, and everything's changed, and I'm changed, and I can't tell what's my name, or who I am!"

The bystanders began now to look at each other, nod, wink significantly, and tap their fingers against their foreheads. There was a whisper, also,

15. tory: person loyal to England during the Revolutionary War.

about securing the gun, and keeping the old fellow from doing mischief; at the very suggestion of which, the self-important man with the cocked hat retired with some precipitation. At this critical moment a fresh, comely woman pressed through the throng to get a peep at the gray-bearded man. She had a chubby child in her arms, which, frightened at his looks, began to cry. "Hush, Rip," cried she, "hush, you little fool; the old man won't hurt you." The name of the child, the air of the mother, the tone of her voice, all awakened a train of recollections in his mind.

"What is your name, my good woman?" asked he.

"Judith Gardenier."

"And your father's name?"

"Ah, poor man, Rip Van Winkle was his name, but it's twenty years since he went away from home with his gun, and never has been heard of since—his dog came home without him; but whether he shot himself, or was carried away by the Indians, nobody can tell. I was then but a little girl."

Rip had but one more question to ask, but he put it with a faltering voice:

"Where's your mother?"

"Oh, she, too, had died but a short time since; she broke a blood-vessel in a fit of passion at a New England peddler."

There was a drop of comfort, at least, in this intelligence. The honest man could contain himself no longer. He caught his daughter and her child in his arms. "I am your father!" cried he—"Young Rip Van Winkle once— old Rip Van Winkle now—Does nobody know poor Rip Van Winkle!"

All stood amazed, until an old woman, tottering out from among the crowd, put her hand to her brow, and peering under it in his face for a moment exclaimed, "Sure enough! It is Rip Van Winkle—it is himself. Welcome home again, old neighbor. Why, where have you been all these twenty long years?"

Rip's story was soon told, for the whole twenty years had been to him but as one night. The neighbors stared when they heard it; some were seen to wink at each other, and put their tongues in their cheeks.

It was determined, however, to take the opinion of old Peter Vanderdonk. Peter was the most ancient inhabitant of the village, and well versed in all the wonderful events and traditions of the neighborhood. He recollected Rip at once, and corroborated his story in the most satisfactory manner. He assured the company that it was a fact, handed down from his ancestor, the historian, that the Kaatskill Mountains had always been haunted by strange beings. That it was affirmed that the great Hendrick Hudson, the first discoverer of the river and country, kept a kind of vigil there every twenty years, with his crew of the *Halfmoon*.[16] That his father had once seen them in their old Dutch dresses playing at ninepins in a hollow of the mountain; and that he himself

---

16. *Halfmoon*: Hudson's ship.

had heard, one summer afternoon, the sound of their balls, like distant peals of thunder.

To make a long story short, the company broke up, and returned to the more important concerns of the election. Rip's daughter took him home to live with her; she had a snug, well-furnished house, and a stout cheery farmer for a husband, whom Rip recollected for one of the urchins that used to climb upon his back. As to Rip's son and heir, who was the ditto of himself, seen leaning against the tree, he was employed to work on the farm; but evinced an hereditary disposition to attend to anything else but his business.

Rip now resumed his old walks and habits; he soon found many of his former cronies, though all rather the worse for the wear and tear of time.

It was some time before he could get into the regular track of gossip, or could be made to comprehend the strange events that had taken place during his torpor.[17] How that there had been a Revolutionary War—that the country had thrown off the yoke of old England—and that, instead of being a subject of His Majesty George the Third, he was now a free citizen of the United States. Rip, in fact, was no politician; the changes of states and empires made but little impression on him; but there was one species of despotism[18] under which he had long groaned, and that was—petticoat government. Happily, that was at an end;

he had got his neck out of the yoke of matrimony, and could go in and out whenever he pleased without dreading the tyranny of Dame Van Winkle. Whenever her name was mentioned, however, he shook his head, shrugged his shoulders, and cast up his eyes; which might pass either for an expression of resignation to his fate, or joy at his deliverance.

He used to tell his story to every stranger that arrived at Mr. Doolittle's hotel. He was observed, at first, to vary on some points every time he told it, which was, doubtless, owing to his having so recently awaked. It at last settled down precisely to the tale I have related, and not a man, woman, or child in the neighborhood but knew it by heart. Some always pretended to doubt the reality of it, and insisted that Rip had been out of his head, and that this was one point on which he always remained flighty. The old Dutch inhabitants, however, almost universally gave it full credit. Even to this day, they never hear a thunderstorm of a summer afternoon about the Kaatskills, but they say Hendrick Hudson and his crew are at their game of ninepins; and it is a common wish of all henpecked husbands in the neighborhood, when life hangs heavy on their hands, that they might have a quieting draught out of Rip Van Winkle's flagon.

---

17. **torpor:** sleep.
18. **despotism:** dictatorship.

A secret is something kept from others or shared only with a few. Whom would you trust with a very important secret? In this short story set in Canada during the early 1900s, Pierre, the driver of a milk wagon, shares a secret with his horse Joseph. Look for clues to help you discover their special secret.

A Secret for Two

Quentin Reynolds (1902–1965)

Montreal is a very large city, but, like all large cities, it has some very small streets. Streets, for instance, like Prince Edward Street, which is only four blocks long, ending in a cul de sac.[1] No one knew Prince Edward Street as well as did Pierre Dupin, for Pierre had delivered milk to the families on the street for thirty years now.

During the past fifteen years the horse which drew the milk wagon used by Pierre was a large white horse named Joseph. In Montreal, especially in that part of Montreal which is very French, the animals, like children, are often given the names of saints. When the big white horse first came to the Provincale Milk Company he didn't have a name. They told Pierre that he could use the white horse henceforth. Pierre stroked the softness of the horse's neck; he stroked the sheen of its splendid belly and he looked into the eyes of the horse.

"This is a kind horse, a gentle and a faithful horse," Pierre said, "and I can see a beautiful spirit shining out of the eyes of the horse. I will name him after good St. Joseph, who was also kind and gentle and faithful and a beautiful spirit."

---

1. **cul de sac:** a dead-end street.

Within a year Joseph knew the milk route as well as Pierre. Pierre used to boast that he didn't need reins—he never touched them. Each morning Pierre arrived at the stables of the Provincale Milk Company at five o'clock. The wagon would be loaded and Joseph hitched to it. Pierre would call "*Bon jour, vieille ami,*"[2] as he climbed into his seat and Joseph would turn his head and the other drivers would smile and say that the horse would smile at Pierre. Then Jacques, the foreman, would say, "All right, Pierre, go on," and Pierre would call softly to Joseph, "*Avance, mon ami,*" and this splendid combination would stalk proudly down the street.

The wagon, without any direction from Pierre, would roll three blocks down St. Catherine Street, then turn right two blocks along Roslyn Avenue; then left, for that was Prince Edward Street. The horse would stop at the first house, allow Pierre perhaps thirty seconds to get down from his seat and put a bottle of milk at the front door and would then go on, skipping two houses and stopping at the third. So down the length of the street. Then Joseph, still without any direction from Pierre, would turn around and come back along the other side. Yes, Joseph was a smart horse.

Pierre would boast at the stable of Joseph's skill. "I never touch the reins. He knows just where to stop. Why, a blind man could handle my route with Joseph pulling the wagon."

So it went on for years—always the same. Pierre and Joseph both grew old together, but gradually, not suddenly. Pierre's huge walrus mustache was pure white now and Joseph didn't lift his knees so high or raise his head as much. Jacques, the foreman of the stables, never noticed that they were both getting old until Pierre appeared one morning carrying a heavy walking stick.

2. *Bon jour, vieille ami*: Good morning, old friend.

"Hey, Pierre," Jacques laughed. "Maybe you got the gout, hey?"

"*Mais oui,*[3] *Jacques,*" Pierre said a bit uncertainly. "One grows old. One's legs get tired."

"You should teach that horse to carry the milk to the front door for you," Jacques told him. "He does everything else."

He knew every one of the forty families he served on Prince Edward Street. The cooks knew that Pierre could neither read nor write, so instead of following the usual custom of leaving a note in an empty bottle if an additional quart of milk was needed they would sing out when they heard the rumble of his wagon wheels over the cobbled street, "Bring an extra quart this morning, Pierre."

"So you have company for dinner tonight," he would call back gaily.

Pierre had a remarkable memory. When he arrived at the stable he'd always remember to tell Jacques, "The Paquins took an extra quart this morning; the Lemoines bought a pint of cream."

Jacques would note these things in a little book he always carried. Most of the drivers had to make out the weekly bills and collect the money, but Jacques, liking Pierre, had always excused him from this task. All Pierre had to do was to arrive at five in the morning, walk to his wagon, which was always in the same spot at the curb, and deliver his milk. He returned some two hours later, got down stiffly from his seat, called a cheery "*Au 'voir*"[4] to Jacques, and then limped slowly down the street.

One morning the president of the Provincale Milk Company came to inspect the early morning deliveries. Jacques pointed Pierre out to him and said: "Watch how he talks to that horse. See how the horse listens and how he turns his head toward Pierre? See the look in that horse's eyes? You know, I think those two share a secret. I have often noticed it. It is as though they both sometimes chuckle at us as they go off on their route. Pierre is a good man, Monsieur President, but he gets old. Would it be too bold of me to suggest that he be retired and be given perhaps a small pension?" he added anxiously.

"But of course," the president laughed. "I know his record. He has been on this route now for thirty years and never once has there been a complaint. Tell him it is time he rested. His salary will go on just the same."

But Pierre refused to retire. He was panic-stricken at the thought of not driving Joseph every day. "We are two old men," he said to Jacques. "Let us wear out together. When Joseph is ready to retire—then I, too, will quit."

Jacques, who was a kind man, understood. There was something about Pierre and Joseph which made a man smile tenderly. It was as though each drew some hidden strength from the other. When Pierre was sitting in his seat, and when Joseph was hitched

---

3. *mais oui*: but yes.
4. *au 'voir*: good-bye.

to the wagon, neither seemed old. But when they finished their work, then Pierre would limp down the street slowly, seeming very old indeed, and the horse's head would drop and he would walk very wearily to his stall.

Then one morning Jacques had dreadful news for Pierre when he arrived. It was a cold morning and still pitch-dark. The air was like iced wine that morning and the snow which had fallen during the night glistened like a million diamonds piled together.

Jacques said, "Pierre, your horse, Joseph, did not wake up this morning. He was very old, Pierre, he was twenty-five and that is like being seventy-five for a man."

"Yes," Pierre said slowly. Yes, I am seventy-five. And I cannot see Joseph again."

"Of course you can," Jacques soothed. "He is over in his stall, looking very peaceful. Go over and see him."

Pierre took one step forward, then turned. "No...no...you don't understand, Jacques."

Jacques clapped him on the shoulder. "We'll find another horse just as good as Joseph. Why, in a month you'll teach him to know your route as well as Joseph did. We'll..."

The look in Pierre's eyes stopped him. For years Pierre had worn a heavy cap, the peak of which came low over his eyes, keeping the bitter morning wind out of them. Now Jacques looked into Pierre's eyes and he saw something which startled him. He saw a dead,

lifeless look in them. The eyes were mirroring the grief that was in Pierre's heart and his soul. It was as though his heart and soul had died.

"Take today off, Pierre," Jacques said, but already Pierre was hobbling off down the street, and had one been near one would have seen tears streaming down his cheeks and have heard half-smothered sobs. Pierre walked to the corner and stepped into the street. There was a warning yell from the driver of a huge truck that was coming fast and there was the scream of brakes, but Pierre apparently heard neither.

Five minutes later an ambulance driver said, "He's dead. Was killed instantly."

Jacques and several of the milk wagon drivers had arrived and they looked down at the still figure.

"I couldn't help it," the driver of the truck protested, "he walked right into my truck. He never saw it, I guess. Why, he walked into it as though he were blind."

The ambulance doctor bent down. "Blind? Of course the man was blind. See those cataracts?[5] This man has been blind for five years." He turned to Jacques, "You say he worked for you? Didn't you know he was blind?"

"No...no..." Jacques said softly. "None of us knew. Only one knew—a friend of his named Joseph.... It was a secret, I think, just between those two."

---

5. **cataracts:** clouding of the lenses of the eyes.

Have you ever planned something carefully only to have everything go wrong? That is what happens in "The Ransom of Red Chief" by O. Henry. Like many of O. Henry's short stories, this one has a surprise ending. Before you read, guess what the story is about from its title. As you read the story, try to figure out how it will end.

The Ransom of Red Chief

O. Henry (1862–1910)

It looked like a good thing: but wait till I tell you. We were down South, in Alabama—Bill Driscoll and myself—when this kidnapping idea struck us. It was, as Bill afterward expressed it, "during a moment of temporary mental apparition";[1] but we didn't find that out till later.

There was a town down there, as flat as a flannel-cake, and called Summit, of course. It contained inhabitants of as undeleterious[2] and self-satisfied a class of peasantry as ever clustered around a Maypole.

Bill and me had a joint capital of about six hundred dollars, and we needed just two thousand dollars more to pull off a fraudulent town-lot scheme in Western Illinois with. We talked it over on the front steps of the Hotel. Philoprogenitiveness,[3] says we, is strong in semi-rural communities; therefore, and for other reasons, a kidnapping project ought to do better there than in the radius of newspapers that send reporters out in plain clothes to stir up talk about such things. We knew that Summit couldn't get after us with anything stronger than constables

---

1. **apparition:** ghost; actually he meant a mental aberration, a mental lapse.
2. **undeleterious:** harmless.
3. **philoprogenitiveness:** love of one's children.

and, maybe, some lackadaisical blood-hounds and a diatribe or two in the *Weekly Farmers' Budget*. So, it looked good.

We selected for our victim the only child of a prominent citizen named Ebenezer Dorset. The father was respectable and tight, a mortgage fancier[4] and a stern, upright collection-plate passer and forecloser. The kid was a boy of ten, with bas-relief freckles, and hair the color of the cover of the magazine you buy at the news-stand when you want to catch a train. Bill and me figured that Ebenezer would melt down for a ransom of two thousands dollars to a cent. But wait till I tell you.

About two miles from Summit was a little mountain, covered with a dense cedar brake. On the rear elevation of this mountain was a cave. There we stored provisions.

One evening after sundown, we drove in a buggy past old Dorset's house. The kid was in the street, throwing rocks at a kitten on the opposite fence.

"Hey, little boy!" says Bill, "would you like to have a bag of candy and a nice ride?"

The boy catches Bill neatly in the eye with a piece of brick.

"That will cost the old man an extra five hundred dollars," says Bill, climbing up over the wheel.

That boy put up a fight like a welter-weight cinnamon bear; but, at last, we got him down in the bottom of the buggy and drove away. We took him up to the cave, and I hitched the horse in the cedar brake. After dark I drove the buggy to the little village, three miles away, where we had hired it, and walked back to the mountain.

Bill was pasting court-plaster over the scratches and bruises on his features. There was a fire burning behind the big rock at the entrance of the cave, and the boy was watching a pot of boiling coffee, with two buzzard tail-feathers stuck in his red hair. He points a stick at me when I come up, and says:

"Ha! cursed paleface, do you dare to enter the camp of Red Chief, the terror of the plains?"

"He's all right now," says Bill, rolling up his trousers and examining some bruises on his shins. "We're playing Indian. We're making Buffalo Bill's show look like magic-lantern views of Palestine in the town hall. I'm Old Hank, the Trapper, Red Chief's captive, and I'm to be scalped at daybreak. By Geronimo! that kid can kick hard."

Yes, sir, that boy seemed to be having the time of his life. The fun of camping out in a cave had made him forget that he was a captive himself. He immediately christened me Snake-eye, the Spy, and announced that, when his braves returned from the warpath, I was to be broiled at the stake at the rising of the sun.

Then we had supper; and he filled his mouth full of bacon and bread and

---

4. **fancier:** person with special interests; actually he meant a financier, a person good with money.

gravy, and began to talk. He made a during-dinner speech something like this:

"I like this fine. I never camped out before; but I had a pet 'possum once, and I was nine last birthday. I hate to go to school. Rats ate up sixteen of Jimmy Talbot's aunt's speckled hen's eggs. Are there any real Indians in these woods? I want some more gravy. Does the trees moving make the wind blow? We had five puppies. What makes your nose so red, Hank? My father has lots of money. Are the stars hot? I whipped Ed Walker twice, Saturday. I don't like girls. You dassent catch toads unless with a string. Do oxen make any noise? Why are oranges round? Have you got beds to sleep on in this cave? Amos Murray has got six toes. A parrot can talk, but a monkey or a fish can't. How many does it take to make twelve?"

Every few minutes he would remember that he was a pesky redskin, and pick up his stick rifle and tiptoe to the mouth of the cave to rubber for the scouts of the hated paleface. Now and then he would let out a war-whoop that made Old Hank the Trapper shiver. That boy had Bill terrorized from the start.

"Red Chief," says I to the kid, "would you like to go home?"

"Aw, what for?" says he. "I don't have any fun at home. I hate to go to school. I like to camp out. You won't take me back home again, Snake-eye, will you?"

"Not right away," says I. "We'll stay here in the cave awhile."

"All right!" says he. "That'll be fine. I never had such fun in all my life."

We went to bed about eleven o'clock. We spread down some wide blankets and quilts and put Red Chief between us. We weren't afraid he'd run away. He kept us awake for three hours, jumping up and reaching for his rifle and screeching: "Hist! pard," in mine and Bill's ears, as the fancied crackle of a twig or the rustle of a leaf revealed to his young imagination the stealthy approach of the outlaw band. At last, I fell into a troubled sleep, and dreamed that I had been kidnapped and chained to a tree by a ferocious pirate with red hair.

Just at daybreak, I was awakened by a series of awful screams from Bill. They weren't yells, or howls, or shouts, or whoops, or yawps, such as you'd expect from a manly set of vocal organs—they were simply indecent, terrifying, humiliating screams, such as women emit when they see ghosts or caterpillars. It's an awful thing to hear a strong, desperate, fat man scream incontinently in a cave at daybreak.

I jumped up to see what the matter was. Red Chief was sitting on Bill's chest, with one hand twined in Bill's hair. In the other he had the sharp case-knife we used for slicing bacon; and he was industriously and realistically trying to take Bill's scalp, according to the sentence that had been pronounced upon him the evening before.

I got the knife away from the kid and made him lie down again. But, from that moment, Bill's spirit was broken. He laid down on his side of the bed, but he never closed an eye again in sleep as long as that boy was with us. I dozed off for a while, but along toward sun-up I remembered that Red Chief had said I was to be burned at the stake at the rising of the sun. I wasn't nervous or afraid; but I sat up and lit my pipe and leaned against a rock.

"What are you getting up so soon for, Sam?" asked Bill.

"Me?" says I. "Oh, I got a kind of pain in my shoulder. I thought sitting up would rest it."

"You're a liar!" says Bill. "You're afraid. You was to be burned at sunrise, and you was afraid he'd do it. And he would, too, if he could find a match. Ain't it awful, Sam? Do you think anybody will pay out money to get a little imp like that back home?"

"Sure," said I. "A rowdy kid like that is just the kind that parents dote on. Now, you and the Chief get up and cook breakfast, while I go up on the top of this mountain and reconnoitre."[5]

I went up on the peak of the little mountain and ran my eye over the contiguous vicinity. Over towards Summit I expected to see the sturdy yeomanry of the village armed with scythes and pitchforks beating the countryside for the dastardly kidnappers. But what I saw was a peaceful landscape dotted with one man ploughing with a dun mule. Nobody was dragging the creek; no couriers dashed hither and yon, bringing tidings of no news to the distracted parents. There was a sylvan attitude of somnolent sleepiness pervading that section of the external outward surface of Alabama that lay exposed to my view. "Perhaps," says I to myself, "it has not yet been discovered that the

---

5. **reconnoitre:** examine the situation.

wolves have borne away the tender lambkin from the fold. Heaven help the wolves!" says I, and I went down the mountain to breakfast.

When I got to the cave I found Bill backed up against the side of it, breathing hard, and the boy threatening to smash him with a rock half as big as a cocoanut.

"He put a red-hot boiled potato down my back." explained Bill, "and then mashed it with his foot; and I boxed his ears. Have you got a gun about you, Sam?"

I took the rock away from the boy and kind of patched up the argument. "I'll fix you," says the kid to Bill. "No man ever yet struck the Red Chief but he got paid for it. You better beware!"

After breakfast the kid takes a piece of leather with strings wrapped around it out of his pocket and goes outside the cave unwinding it.

"What's he up to now?" says Bill, anxiously. "You don't think he'll run away, do you Sam?"

"No fear of it," says I. "He don't seem to be much of a home body. But we've got to fix up some plan about the ransom. There don't seem to be much excitement around Summit on account of his disappearance; but maybe they haven't realized yet that he's gone. His folks may think he's spending the night with Aunt Jane or one of the neighbors. Anyhow, he'll be missed today. Tonight we must get a message to his father demanding the two thousand dollars for his return."

Just then we heard a kind of war-whoop, such as David might have emitted when he knocked out the champion Goliath. It was a sling that Red Chief had pulled out of his pocket, and he was whirling it around his head.

I dodged, and heard a heavy thud and a kind of sigh from Bill, like a horse gives out when you take his saddle off. A rock the size of an egg had caught Bill just behind his left ear. He loosened himself all over and fell in the fire across the frying pan of hot water for washing the dishes. I dragged him out and poured cold water on his head for half an hour.

By and by, Bill sits up and feels behind his ear and says: "Sam, do you know who my favorite Biblical character is?"

"Take it easy," says I. "You'll come to your senses presently."

"King Herod," says he. "You won't go away and leave me here alone, will you, Sam?"

I went out and caught that boy and shook him until his freckles rattled.

"If you don't behave," says I, "I'll take you straight home. Now, are you going to be good, or not?"

"I was only funning," says he, sullenly. "I didn't mean to hurt Old Hank. But what did he hit me for? I'll behave, Snake-eye, if you won't send me home, and if you'll let me play the Black Scout today."

"I don't know the game," says I. "That's for you and Mr. Bill to decide. He's your playmate for the day. I'm

going away for a while, on business. Now, you come in and make friends with him and say you are sorry for hurting him, or home you go, at once."

I made him and Bill shake hands, and then I took Bill aside and told him I was going to Poplar Grove, a little village three miles from the cave, and find out what I could about how the kidnapping had been regarded in Summit. Also, I thought it best to send a peremptory letter to old man Dorset that day, demanding the ransom and dictating how it should be paid.

"You know, Sam," says Bill, "I've stood by you without batting an eye in earthquakes, fire and flood—in poker games, dynamite outrages, police raids, train robberies, and cyclones. I

never lost my nerve yet till we kidnapped that two-legged skyrocket of a kid. He's got me going. You won't leave me long with him, will you, Sam?"

"I'll be back some time this afternoon," says I. "You must keep the boy amused and quiet till I return. And now we'll write the letter to old Dorset."

Bill and I got paper and pencil and worked on the letter while Red Chief, with a blanket wrapped around him, strutted up and down, guarding the mouth of the cave. Bill begged me tearfully to make the ransom fifteen hundred dollars instead of two thousand. "I ain't attempting," says he, "to decry[6] the celebrated moral aspect

---

6. **decry**: underestimate.

of parental affection, but we're dealing with humans, and it ain't human for anybody to give up two thousand dollars for that forty-pound chunk of freckled wildcat. I'm willing to take a chance at fifteen hundred dollars. You can charge the difference up to me."

So, to relieve Bill, I acceded, and we collaborated a letter that ran this way:

EBENEZER DORSET, ESQ.:

We have your boy concealed in a place far from Summit. It is useless for you or the most skillful detectives to attempt to find him. Absolutely, the only terms on which you can have him restored to you are these: We demand fifteen hundred dollars in large bills for his return; the money to be left at midnight tonight at the same spot and in the same box as your reply as hereinafter described. If you agree to these terms, send your answer in writing by a solitary messenger tonight at half-past eight o'clock. After crossing Owl Creek on the road to Poplar Grove, there are three large trees about a hundred yards apart, close to the fence of the wheat field on the right-hand side. At the bottom of the fence-post, opposite the third tree, will be found a small pasteboard box.

The messenger will place the answer in this box and return immediately to Summit.

If you attempt any treachery or fail to comply with our demand as stated, you will never see your boy again.

If you pay the money as demanded, he will be returned to you safe and well within three hours. These terms are final, and if you do not accede to them no further communication will be attempted.

TWO DESPERATE MEN

I addressed this letter to Dorset, and put it in my pocket. As I was about to start, the kid comes up to me and says:

"Aw, Snake-eye, you said I could play the Black Scout while you was gone."

"Play it, of course," says I. "Mr. Bill will play with you. What kind of a game is it?"

"I'm the Black Scout," says Red Chief, "and I have to ride to the stockade to warn the settlers that the Indians are coming. I'm tired of playing Indian myself. I want to be the Black Scout."

"All right," says I. "It sounds harmless to me. I guess Mr. Bill will help you foil the pesky savages."

"What am I to do?" asks Bill, looking at the kid suspiciously.

"You are the hoss," says Black Scout. "Get down on your hands and knees. How can I ride to the stockade without a hoss?"

"You'd better keep him interested," said I, "till we get the scheme going. Loosen up."

Bill gets down on his all fours, and a look comes in his eye like a rabbit's when you catch it in a trap.

"How far is it to the stockade, kid?" he asks, in a husky manner of voice.

"Ninety miles," says the Black Scout. "And you have to hump yourself to get there on time. Whoa, now!"

The Black Scout jumps on Bill's back and digs his heels in his side.

"For Heaven's sake," says Bill, "hurry back, Sam, as soon as you can. I wish we hadn't made the ransom more than a thousand. Say, you quit kicking me or I'll get up and warm you good."

I walked over to Poplar Grove and sat around the post-office and store, talking with the chaw-bacons that came in to trade. One whiskerando says that he hears Summit is all upset on account of Elder Ebenezer Dorset's boy having been lost or stolen. That was all I wanted to know. I bought some smoking tobacco, referred casually to the price of black-eyed peas, posted my letter surreptitiously,[7] and came away. The postmaster said the mail-carrier would come by in an hour to take the mail to Summit.

When I got back to the cave Bill and the boy were not to be found. I explored the vicinity of the cave, and risked a yodel or two, but there was no response.

So I lighted my pipe and sat down on a mossy bank to await developments.

In about half an hour I heard the bushes rustle, and Bill wabbled out into the little glade in front of the cave. Behind him was the kid, stepping softly like a scout, with a broad grin on his face. Bill stopped, took off his hat, and wiped his face with a red handkerchief. The kid stopped about eight feet behind him.

"Sam," says Bill, "I suppose you'll think I'm a renegade, but I couldn't help it. I'm a grown person with masculine proclivities and habits of self-defense, but there is a time when all systems of egotism and predominance fail. The boy is gone. I sent him home. All is off. There was martyrs in old times," goes on Bill, "that suffered death rather than give up the particular graft they enjoyed. None of 'em ever was subjugated[8] to such supernatural tortures as I have been. I tried to be faithful to our articles of depredation; but there came a limit."

"What's the trouble, Bill?" I asks him.

"I was rode," says Bill, "the ninety miles to the stockade, not barring an inch. Then, when the settlers was rescued, I was given oats. Sand ain't a palatable substitute. And then, for an hour I had to try to explain to him why there was nothin' in holes, how a road can run both ways, and what makes the grass green. I tell you, Sam, a human can only stand so much. I takes him by the neck of his clothes and drags him down the mountain. On the way he kicks my legs black and blue from the knees down; and I've got to have two or three bites on my thumb and hand cauterized.

"But he's gone"—continues Bill—"gone home. I showed him the road to Summit and kicked him about eight feet nearer there at one kick. I'm sorry we lose the ransom; but it was either that or Bill Driscoll to the madhouse."

---

7. **surreptitiously:** secretly.
8. **subjugated:** enslaved; actually he meant subjected.

Bill is puffing and blowing, but there is a look of ineffable peace and growing content on his rose-pink features.

"Bill," says I, "there isn't any heart disease in your family, is there?"

"No," says Bill, "nothing chronic except malaria and accidents. Why?"

"Then you might turn around," says I, "and have a look behind you."

Bill turns and sees the boy, and loses his complexion and sits down plump on the ground and begins to pluck aimlessly at grass and little sticks. For an hour I was afraid of his mind. And then I told him that my scheme was to put the whole job through immediately and that we would get the ransom and be off with it by midnight if old Dorset fell in with our proposition. So Bill braced up enough to give the kid a weak sort of a smile and a promise to play the Russian in a Japanese war with him as soon as he felt a little better.

I had a scheme for collecting that ransom without danger of being caught by counterplots that ought to commend itself to professional kidnappers. The tree under which the answer was to be left—and the money later on—was close to the road fence with big, bare fields on all sides. If a gang of constables should be watching for any one to come for the note, they could see him a long way off crossing the fields or in the road. But no, sirree! At half-past eight I was up in that tree as well hidden as a tree toad, waiting for the messenger to arrive.

Exactly on time, a half-grown boy rides up the road on a bicycle, locates the pasteboard box at the foot of the fence-post, slips a folded piece of paper into it, and pedals away again back to toward Summit.

I waited an hour and then concluded the thing was square. I slid down the tree, got the note, slipped along the fence till I struck the woods, and was back at the cave in another half an hour. I opened the note, got near the lantern, and read it to Bill. It was written with a pen in a crabbed hand, and the sum and substance of it was this:

TWO DESPERATE MEN
Gentlemen:
    I received your letter today by post, in regard to the ransom you ask for the return of my son. I think you are a little high in your demands, and I hereby make you a counter-proposition, which I am inclined to believe you will accept. You bring Johnny home and pay me two hundred and fifty dollars in cash, and I agree to take him off your hands. You had better come at night, for the neighbors believe he is lost, and I couldn't be responsible for what they would do to anybody they saw bringing him back.

        Very respectfully,
        Ebenezer Dorset

"Great Pirates of Penzance," says I; "of all the impudent—"

But I glanced at Bill, and hesitated. He had the most appealing look in his eyes I ever saw on the face of a dumb or a talking brute.

"Sam," says he, "what's two hundred fifty dollars, after all? We've got the money. One more night of this kid will send me to a bed in Bedlam. Besides being a thorough gentlemen, I think Mr. Dorset is a spendthrift[9] for making us such a liberal offer. You ain't going to let the chance go, are you?"

"Tell you the truth, Bill," says I, "this little he ewe lamb has somewhat got on my nerves too. We'll take him home, pay the ransom, and make our getaway."

We took him home that night. We got him to go by telling him that his father had bought a silver-mounted rifle and a pair of moccasins for him, and we were to hunt bears the next day.

It was just twelve o'clock when we knocked at Ebenezer's front door. Just at the moment when I should have been abstracting the fifteen hundred dollars from the box under the tree, according to the original proposition, Bill was counting out two hundred and fifty dollars into Dorset's hand.

When the kid found out we were going to leave him at home he started up a howl like a calliope and fastened himself as tight as a leech to Bill's leg. His father peeled him away gradually, like a porous plaster.

"How long can you hold him?" asks Bill.

"I'm not as strong as I used to be," says old Dorset, "but I think I can promise you ten minutes."

"Enough," says Bill. "In ten minutes I shall cross the Central,

Southern, and Middle Western States, and be legging it trippingly for the Canadian border."

And, as dark as it was, and as fat as Bill was, and as good a runner as I am, he was a good mile and a half out of Summit before I could catch up with him.

9. **spendthrift:** overly generous person.

Edgar Allan Poe believed that a short story should have a great impact on its readers. In "The Tell-Tale Heart," Poe carefully selected each detail to build suspense and to create horror as more and more of the narrator's thoughts and actions are revealed. As you read this story, try to figure out what makes the narrator so "dreadfully nervous."

The Tell-Tale Heart

Edgar Allan Poe (1809–1849)

True!—nervous—very, very dreadfully nervous I had been and am; but why *will* you say that I am mad?[1] The disease had sharpened my senses—not destroyed—not dulled them. Above all was the sense of hearing acute.[2] I heard all things in the heaven and in the earth. I heard many things in hell. How, then, am I mad? Hearken! and observe how healthily—how calmly I can tell you the whole story.

It is impossible to say how first the idea entered my brain; but once conceived, it haunted me day and night. Object there was none. Passion there was none. I loved the old man. He had never wronged me. He had never given me insult. For his gold I had no desire. I think it was his eye! yes, it was this! One of his eyes resembled that of a vulture—a pale blue eye, with a film over it. Whenever it fell upon me, my blood ran cold; and so by degrees—very gradually—I made up my mind to take the life of the old man, and thus rid myself of the eye for ever.

Now this is the point. You fancy me mad. Madmen know nothing. But you should have seen *me*. You should have seen how wisely I proceeded—with

1. **mad:** insane.
2. **acute:** sharp.

what caution—with what foresight—with what dissimulation[3] I went to work! I was never kinder to the old man than during the whole week before I killed him. And every night, about midnight, I turned the latch of his door and opened it—oh, so gently! And then, when I had made an opening sufficient for my head, I put in a dark lantern, all closed, closed, so that no light shone out, and then I thrust in my head. Oh, you would have laughed to see how cunningly I thrust it in! I moved it slowly—very, very slowly, so that I might not disturb the old man's sleep. It took me an hour to place my whole head within the opening so far that I could see him as he lay upon his bed. Ha!—would a madman have been so wise as this? And then, when my head was well in the room, I undid the lantern cautiously—oh, so cautiously—cautiously (for the hinges creaked)—I undid it just so much that a single thin ray fell upon the vulture eye. And this I did for seven long nights—every night just at midnight—but I found the eye always closed; and so it was impossible to do the work; for it was not the old man who vexed[4] me, but his Evil Eye. And every morning, when the day broke, I went boldly into the chamber, and spoke courageously to him, calling him by name in a hearty tone, and inquiring how he had passed the night. So you see he would have been a very profound old man, indeed, to suspect that every night, just at twelve, I looked in upon him while he slept.

Upon the eighth night I was more than usually cautious in opening the door. A watch's minute hand moves more quickly than did mine. Never before that night had I *felt* the extent of my own powers—of my sagacity.[5] I could scarcely contain my feelings of triumph. To think that there I was, opening the door, little by little, and he not even to dream of my secret deeds or thoughts. I fairly chuckled at the idea; and perhaps he heard me; for he moved on the bed suddenly, as if startled. Now you may think that I drew back—but no. His room was as black as pitch with the thick darkness (for the shutters were close fastened, through fear of robbers), and so I knew that he could not see the opening of the door, and I kept pushing it on steadily, steadily.

I had my head in, and was about to open the lantern, when my thumb slipped upon the tin fastening, and the old man sprang up in the bed, crying out—"Who's there?"

I kept quite still and said nothing. For a whole hour I did not move a muscle, and in the meantime I did not hear him lie down. He was still sitting up in the bed listening;—just as I have done, night after night, hearkening to the death watches[6] in the wall.

Presently I heard a slight groan, and I knew it was the groan of mortal terror. It was not a groan of pain or of grief—oh, no!—it was the low stifled sound that arises from the bottom of the soul when overcharged with awe. I knew the sound well. Many a night,

---

3. **dissimulation:** false pretense.
4. **vexed:** troubled.
5. **sagacity:** wisdom.
6. **death watches:** small insects that make a ticking sound; superstition says the ticking warns of death.

just at midnight, when all the world slept, it has welled up from my own bosom, deepening, with its dreadful echo, the terrors that distracted me. I say I knew it well. I knew what the old man felt, and pitied him, although I chuckled at heart. I knew that he had been lying awake ever since the first slight noise, when he had turned in the bed. His fears had been ever since growing upon him. He had been trying to fancy them causeless, but could not. He had been saying to himself—"It is nothing but the wind in the chimney—it is only a mouse crossing the floor," or "it is merely a cricket which has made a single chirp." Yes, he has been trying to comfort himself with these suppositions; but he had found all in vain. *All in vain;* because Death, in approaching him, had stalked with his black shadow before him, and enveloped the victim. And it was the mournful influence of the unperceived shadow that caused him to feel—although he neither saw nor heard—to *feel* the presence of my head within the room.

When I had waited a long time, very patiently, without hearing him lie down, I resolved to open a little—a very, very little crevice in the lantern. So I opened it—you cannot imagine how stealthily,[7] stealthily—until, at length, a single dim ray, like the thread of the spider, shot from out the crevice and full upon the vulture eye.

It was open—wide, wide open—and I grew furious as I gazed upon it. I saw it with perfect distinctness—all a dull blue, with a hideous veil over it that chilled the very marrow in my

Specified illustration by Fritz Eichenberg. From *Tales of Edgar Allan Poe*, Illustrated by Fritz Eichenberg. Copyright 1944 and renewed 1972 by Random House, Inc. Reprinted by permission of the publisher.

bones; but I could see nothing else of the old man's face or person: for I had directed the ray as if by instinct, precisely upon the damned spot.

And now have I not told you that what you mistake for madness is but over-acuteness of the senses?—now, I say, there came to my ears a low, dull, quick sound, such as a watch makes when enveloped in cotton. I knew *that* sound well too. It was the beating of the old man's heart. It increased my fury, as the beating of a drum stimulates the soldier into courage.

But even yet I refrained and kept still. I scarcely breathed. I held the

7. **stealthily:** slyly.

lantern motionless. I tried how steadily I could maintain the ray upon the eye. Meantime the hellish tattoo[8] of the heart increased. It grew quicker and quicker, and louder and louder every instant. The old man's terror *must* have been extreme! It grew louder, I say, louder every moment!—you mark me well? I have told you that I am nervous: so I am. And now at the dead hour of the night, amid the dreadful silence of that old house, so strange a noise as this excited me to uncontrollable terror. Yet, for some minutes longer I refrained and stood still. But the beating grew louder, louder! I thought the heart must burst. And now a new anxiety seized me—the sound would be heard by a neighbor! The old man's hour had come! With a loud yell, I threw open the lantern and leaped into the room. He shrieked once—once only. In an instant I dragged him to the floor, and pulled the heavy bed over him. I then smiled gaily, to find the deed so far done. But, for many minutes, the heart beat on with a muffled sound. This, however, did not vex me; it would not be heard through the wall. At length it ceased. The old man was dead. I removed the bed and examined the corpse. Yes, he was stone, stone dead. I placed my hand upon the heart and held it there many minutes. There was no pulsation. He was stone dead. His eye would trouble me no more.

If still you think me mad, you will think so no longer when I describe the wise precautions I took for the concealment of the body. The night waned,[9] and I worked hastily, but in silence. First of all I dismembered the corpse. I cut off the head and the arms and the legs.

I then took up three planks from the flooring of the chamber, and deposited all between the scantlings.[10] I then replaced the boards so cleverly, so cunningly, that no human eye—not even *his*—could have detected any thing wrong. There was nothing to wash out—no stain of any kind—no blood-spot whatever. I had been too wary for that. A tub had caught all—ha! ha!

When I had made an end of these labors, it was four o'clock—still dark as midnight. As the bell sounded the hour, there came a knocking at the street door. I went down to open it with a light heart,—for what had I *now* to fear? There entered three men, who introduced themselves, with perfect suavity, as officers of the police. A shriek had been heard by a neighbor during the night; suspicion of foul play had been aroused; information had been lodged at the police office, and they (the officers) had been deputed to search the premises.

I smiled,—for *what* had I to fear? I bade the gentlemen welcome. The shriek, I said, was my own in a dream. The old man, I mentioned, was absent in the country. I took my visitors all over the house. I bade them search—search *well*. I led them, at length, to *his* chamber. I showed them his treasures,

8. **tattoo:** steady beat.
9. **waned:** ended gradually.
10. **scantlings:** small wooden beams.

secure, undisturbed. In the enthusiasm of my confidence, I brought chairs into the room, and desired them *here* to rest from their fatigues, while I myself, in the wild audacity[11] of my perfect triumph, placed my own seat upon the very spot beneath which reposed the corpse of the victim.

The officers were satisfied. My *manner* had convinced them. I was singularly at ease. They sat, and while I answered cheerily, they chatted familiar things. But, ere long, I felt myself getting pale and wished them gone. My head ached, and I fancied a ringing in my ears: but still they sat and still chatted. The ringing became more distinct:—it continued and became more distinct: I talked more freely to get rid of the feeling: but it continued and gained definitiveness—until, at length, I found that the noise was *not* within my ears.

No doubt I now grew *very* pale;—but I talked more fluently, and with a heightened voice. Yet the sound increased—and what could I do? It was *a low, dull, quick sound—much such a sound as a watch makes when enveloped in cotton.* I gasped for breath—and yet the officers heard it not. I talked more quickly—more vehemently; but the noise steadily increased. I arose and argued about trifles, in a high key and with violent gesticulations,[12] but the noise steadily increased. Why *would* they not be gone? I paced the floor to and fro with heavy strides, as if excited to fury by the observation of the men—but the noise steadily increased. Oh God! what *could* I do? I foamed—I raved—I swore! I swung the chair upon which I had been sitting, and grated it upon the boards, but the noise arose over all and continually increased. It grew louder—louder—*louder!* And still the men chatted pleasantly, and smiled. Was it possible they heard not? Almighty God!—no, no! They heard!—they suspected!—they *knew!*—they were making a mockery of my horror!—this I thought, and this I think. But any thing was better than this agony! Any thing was more tolerable than this derision![13] I could bear those hypocritical smiles no longer! I felt that I must scream or die!—and now—again!—hark! louder! louder! louder! *louder!*—

"Villains!" I shrieked, "dissemble[14] no more! I admit the deed!—tear up the planks!—here, here!—it is the beating of his hideous heart!"

---

11. **audacity**: boldness.
12. **gesticulations**: gestures.
13. **derision**: ridicule.
14. **dissemble**: pretend.

What is your favorite fantasy? Do you imagine yourself a famous person, or do you dream of living in a far-off land? Walter Mitty, the main character in this short story, daydreams often because his everyday life is so routine and frustrating. As you read, look for clues that trigger Walter's daydreams.

The Secret Life of Walter Mitty

James Thurber (1894–1961)

"We're going through!" The Commander's voice was like thin ice breaking. He wore his full-dress uniform, with the heavily braided white cap pulled down rakishly over one cold gray eye. "We can't make it, sir. It's spoiling for a hurricane, if you ask me." "I'm not asking you, Lieutenant Berg," said the Commander. "Throw on the power lights! Rev her up to 8,500! We're going through!" The pounding of the cylinders increased: ta-pocketa-pocketa-pocketa-*pocketa-pocketa*. The Commander stared at the ice forming on the pilot window. He walked over and twisted a row of complicated dials. "Switch on No. 8 auxiliary!" he shouted. "Switch on No. 8 auxiliary!" repeated Lieutenant Berg. "Full strength in No. 3 turret!" shouted the Commander. "Full strength in No. 3 turret!" The crew, bending to their various tasks in the huge, hurtling eight-engined Navy hydroplane, looked at each other and grinned. "The Old Man'll get us through," they said to one another. "The Old Man ain't afraid of Hell!"...

"Not so fast! You're driving too fast!" said Mrs. Mitty. "What are you driving so fast for?"

"Hmm?" said Walter Mitty. He looked at his wife, in the seat beside him, with shocked astonishment. She seemed grossly unfamiliar, like a strange woman who had yelled at him in a crowd. "You were up to fifty-five," she said. "You know I don't like to go more than forty. You were up to fifty-five." Walter Mitty drove on toward Waterbury in silence, the roaring of the SN202 through the worst storm in twenty years of Navy flying fading in the remote, intimate airways of his mind. "You're tensed up again," said Mrs. Mitty. "It's one of your days. I wish you'd let Dr. Renshaw look you over."

Walter Mitty stopped the car in front of the building where his wife went to have her hair done. "Remember to get those overshoes while I'm having my hair done," she said. "I don't need overshoes," said Mitty. She put her mirror back into her bag. "We've been through that," she said, getting out of the car. "You're not a young man any longer." He raced the engine a little. "Why don't you wear your gloves? Have you lost your gloves?" Walter Mitty reached in a pocket and brought out the gloves. He put them on, but after she had turned and gone into the building and he had driven on to a red light, he took them off again. "Pick it up, brother!" snapped a cop as the light changed, and Mitty hastily pulled on his gloves and lurched ahead. He drove around the streets aimlessly for a time, and then he drove past the hospital on his way to the parking lot.

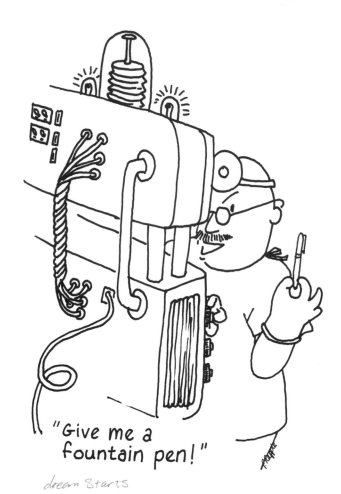

"Give me a fountain pen!"

dream starts

?. . . "It's the millionaire banker, Wellington McMillan," said the pretty nurse. "Yes?" said Walter Mitty, removing his gloves slowly. "Who has the case?" "Dr. Renshaw and Dr. Benbow, but there are two specialists here, Dr. Remington from New York and Dr. Pritchard-Mitford from London. He flew over." A door opened down a long, cool corridor and Dr. Renshaw came out. He looked distraught and haggard.' "Hello, Mitty," he said. "We're having the devil's own time with McMillan, the millionaire banker and close personal

---

1. **distraught and haggard:** extremely upset and exhausted.

friend of Roosevelt. Obstreosis of the ductal tract. Tertiary. Wish you'd take a look at him." "Glad to," said Mitty.

In the operating room there were whispered introductions: "Dr. Remington, Dr. Mitty. Dr. Pritchard-Mitford, Dr. Mitty." "I've read your book on streptothricosis," said Pritchard-Mitford, shaking hands. "A brilliant performance, sir." "Thank you," said Walter Mitty. "Didn't know you were in the states, Mitty," grumbled Remington. "Coals to Newcastle, bringing Mitford and me up here for a tertiary." "You are very kind," said Mitty. A huge, complicated machine, connected to the operating table, with many tubes and wires, began at this moment to go pocketa-pocketa-pocketa. "The new anaesthetizer is giving away!" shouted an intern. "There is no one in the East who knows how to fix it!" "Quiet, man!" said Mitty, in a low, cool voice. He sprang to the machine, which was now going pocketa-pocketa-queep-pocketa-queep. He began fingering delicately a row of glistening dials. "Give me a fountain pen!" he snapped. Someone handed him a fountain pen. He pulled a faulty piston out of the machine and inserted the pen in its place. "That will hold for ten minutes," he said. "Get on with the operation." A nurse hurried over and whispered to Renshaw, and Mitty saw the man turn pale. "Coreopsis has set in," said Renshaw nervously. "If you would take over, Mitty?" Mitty looked at him and at the craven figure of Benbow, who drank, and at the grave, uncertain faces of the two great specialists. "If you wish," he said. They slipped a white gown on him; he adjusted a mask and drew on thin gloves; nurses handed him shining . . .

"Back it up, Mac! Look out for that Buick!" Walter Mitty jammed on the brakes. "Wrong lane, Mac," said the parking-lot attendant, looking at Mitty closely. "Gee. Yeh," muttered Mitty. He began cautiously to back out of the lane marked "Exit Only." "Leave her sit there," said the attendant. "I'll put her away." Mitty got out of the car. "Hey, better leave the key." "Oh," said Mitty, handing the man the ignition key. The attendant vaulted into the car, backed it up with insolent skill, and put it where it belonged.

They're so darn cocky, thought Walter Mitty, walking along Main Street; they think they know everything. Once he had tried to take his chains off, outside New Milford, and he had got them wound around the axles. A man had had to come out in a wrecking car and unwind them, a young, grinning garageman. Since then Mrs. Mitty always made him drive to a garage to have the chains taken off. The next time, he thought, I'll wear my right arm in a sling; they won't grin at me then. I'll have my right arm in a sling and they'll see I couldn't possibly take the chains off myself. He kicked at the slush on the sidewalk. "Overshoes," he said to himself and he began looking for a shoe store.

When he came out into the street again, with the overshoes in a box

"This is my Webley-Vickers 50.80."

under his arm, Walter Mitty began to wonder what the other thing was his wife had told him to get. She had told him twice before they set out from their house for Waterbury. In a way he hated these weekly trips to town—he was always getting something wrong. Kleenex, he thought. Squibb's, razor blades? No. Toothpaste, toothbrush, bicarbonate, carborundum, initiative and referendum? He gave it up. But she would remember it. "Where's the what's-its-name?" she would ask. "Don't tell me you forgot the what's-its-name." A newsboy went by shouting something about the Waterbury trial.

. . . "Perhaps this will refresh your memory." The District Attorney suddenly thrust a heavy automatic at the quiet figure on the witness stand. "Have you ever seen this before?"

Walter Mitty took the gun and examined it expertly. "This is my Webley-Vickers 50.80," he said calmly. An excited buzz ran around the courtroom. The Judge rapped for order. "You are a crack shot with any sort of firearms, I believe?" said the District Attorney, insinuatingly. "Objection!" shouted Mitty's attorney. "We have shown that the defendant could not have fired the shot. We have shown that he wore his right arm in a sling on the night of the fourteenth of July." Walter Mitty raised his hand briefly and the bickering attorneys were stilled. "With any known make of gun," he said evenly, "I could have killed Gregory Fitzhurst at three hundred feet *with my left hand.*" Pandemonium[2] broke loose in the

2. **pandemonium:** chaos, disorder.

courtroom. A woman's scream rose above the bedlam and suddenly a lovely, dark-haired girl was in Walter Mitty's arms. The District Attorney struck at her savagely. Without rising from his chair, Mitty let the man have it on the point of the chin. "You miserable cur!"[3] . . .

"Puppy biscuit," said Walter Mitty. He stopped walking and the buildings of Waterbury rose up out of the misty courtroom and surrounded him again. A woman who was passing laughed. "He said 'Puppy biscuit.'" she said to her companion. "That man said 'Puppy biscuit' to himself." Walter Mitty hurried on. He went into an A. & P., not the first one he came to but a smaller one farther up the street. "I want some biscuit for small, young dogs," he said to the clerk. "Any special brand, sir?" The greatest pistol shot in the world thought a moment. "It says 'Puppies Bark for It' on the box," said Walter Mitty.

His wife would be through at the hairdresser's in fifteen minutes, Mitty saw in looking at his watch, unless they had trouble drying it; sometimes they had trouble drying it. She didn't like to get to the hotel first; she would want him to be there waiting for her as usual. He found a big leather chair in the lobby, facing a window, and he put the overshoes and the puppy biscuit on the floor beside it. He picked up an old copy of *Liberty* and sank down into the chair. "Can Germany Conquer the World Through the Air?" Walter Mitty looked at the pictures of bombing planes and of ruined streets.

. . . "The cannonading has got the wind up in young Raleigh, sir," said the sergeant. Captain Mitty looked up at him through tousled hair. "Get him to bed," he said wearily, "with the others. I'll fly alone." "But you can't, sir," said the sergeant anxiously. "It takes two men to handle that bomber and the Archies are pounding hell out of the air. Von Richtman's circus is between here and Saulier." "Somebody's got to get that ammunition dump," said Mitty. "I'm going over. Spot of brandy?" He poured a drink for the sergeant and one for himself. War thundered and whined around the dugout and battered at the door. There was a rending of wood, and splinters flew through the room. "A bit of a near thing," said Captain Mitty carelessly. "The box barrage is closing in," said

"Somebody's got to get that ammunition dump."

3. cur: dog.

the sergeant. "We only live once, Sergeant," said Mitty, with his faint, fleeting smile. "Or do we?" He poured another brandy and tossed it off. "I never see a man could hold his brandy like you, sir," said the sergeant. "Begging you pardon, sir." Captain Mitty stood up and strapped on his huge Webley-Vickers automatic. "It's forty kilometres through hell, sir," said the sergeant. Mitty finished one last brandy. "After all," he said softly, "what isn't?" The pounding of the cannon increased; there was the rat-tat-tatting of machine guns, and from somewhere came the menacing pocketa-pocketa-pocketa of the new flame throwers. Walter Mitty walked to the door of the dugout humming "Auprès de Ma Blonde." He turned and waved to the sergeant. "Cheerio!" he said....

Something struck his shoulder. "I've been looking all over this hotel for you," said Mrs. Mitty. "Why do you have to hide in this old chair? How did you expect me to find you?" "Things close in," said Walter Mitty vaguely. "What?" Mrs. Mitty said. "Did you get the what's-its-name? The puppy biscuit? What's in that box?" "Over-shoes," said Mitty. "Couldn't you have put them on in the store?" "I was thinking," said Walter Mitty. "Does it ever occur to you that I am sometimes thinking?" She looked at him. "I'm going to take your temperature when I get you home," she said.

They went out through the revolving doors that made a faintly derisive whistling sound when you pushed them. It was two blocks to the parking lot. At the drugstore on the corner she said, "Wait here for me. I forgot something. I won't be a minute." She was more than a minute. Walter Mitty lighted a cigarette. It began to rain, rain with sleet in it. He stood up against the wall of the drugstore smoking.... He put his shoulders back and his heels together. "To hell with the handkerchief," said Walter Mitty scornfully. He took one last drag on his cigarette and snapped it away. Then, with that faint, fleeting smile playing about his lips, he faced the firing squad; erect and motionless, proud and disdainful,⁴ Walter Mitty, the Unde-feated, inscrutable⁵ to the last.

---

4. **disdainful:** scornful.
5. **inscrutable:** mysterious.

Unit 2: Novels

A novel is not just a work of art:
It is somehow a work of life as well.
George P. Elliott

The short stories in the first unit are some of the best in literature. In this unit, you will read excerpts from two novels. A novel is more complex than a short story. It has more characters, more settings, and more twists and turns in its plot. The author of a novel is able to describe the characters, settings, and plot in greater detail.

To keep these details straight, it is helpful to remember all you have experienced. Ask yourself if you know someone like each character. Perhaps you have faced similar problems. Maybe you have visited places like those described in each setting. Relating what you read to what you already know is a powerful tool that will help you remember and understand the novel better.

In the first excerpt, you join two children returning to school. On the very first day, they run into problems with their teacher. In the second excerpt, you visit a farm and watch as the animals take matters into their own hands. Enjoy the excerpts from these popular novels. To find out how each one ends, you may want to read the entire book.

This novel is set in Mississippi in the 1930s before schools were desegregated. The schools for blacks and the schools for whites were supposedly equal, but you will discover that they were not. The main characters are the nine-year-old narrator Cassie; her brother Little Man, who is just starting first grade; their mother, an upper grade teacher in a different building; and Miss Crocker, a lower grade teacher. It is the first day of school, and Miss Crocker is assigning books to her students. Read to find out what upsets Miss Crocker, the children, and their mother.

From

Roll of Thunder, Hear My Cry

Mildred D. Taylor (1943–

By ten o'clock, Miss Crocker had rearranged our seating and written our names on her seating chart. I was still sitting beside Gracey and Alma but we had been moved from the third to the first row in front of a small potbellied stove. Although being eyeball to eyeball with Miss Crocker was nothing to look forward to, the prospect of being warm once the cold weather set in was nothing to be sneezed at either, so I resolved[1] to make the best of my rather dubious[2] position.

Now Miss Crocker made a startling announcement: This year we would all have books.

Everyone gasped, for most of the students had never handled a book at all besides the family Bible. I admit that even I was somewhat excited. Although Mama had several books, I had never had one of my very own.

"Now we're very fortunate to get these readers," Miss Crocker explained

---

1. **resolved:** decided.
2. **dubious:** uncertain.

HER WORLD; Phillip Evergood; 1948; The Metropolitan Museum of Art, Arthur
H. Hearn Fund, 1950. (50.29)

while we eagerly awaited the _uncovering_ unveiling. "The county superintendent of schools himself brought these books down here for our use and we must take extra-good care of them." She moved toward her desk. "So let's all promise that we'll take the best care possible of these new books." She stared down, expecting our response. "All right, all together, let's repeat, 'We promise to take good care of our new books.'" She looked sharply at me as she spoke.

"WE PROMISE TO TAKE GOOD CARE OF OUR NEW BOOKS!"

"Fine," Miss Crocker beamed, then proudly threw back the tarpaulin.

Sitting so close to the desk, I could see that the covers of the books, a motley red, were badly worn and that the gray edges of the pages had been marred by pencils, crayons, and ink. My anticipation at having my own book ebbed to a sinking disappointment. But Miss Crocker continued to beam as she called each fourth grader to her desk and, recording a number in her roll book, handed him or her a book.

As I returned from my trip to her desk, I noticed the first graders anxiously watching the disappearing pile. Miss Crocker must have noticed them too, for as I sat down she said,

"Don't worry, little ones, there are plenty of readers for you too. See there on Miss Davis's desk." Wide eyes turned to the covered teacher's platform directly in front of them and an audible sigh of relief swelled in the room.

I glanced across at Little Man, his face lit in eager excitement. I knew that he could not see the soiled covers or the marred pages from where he sat, and even though his penchant[3] for cleanliness was often annoying, I did not like to think of his disappointment when he saw the books as they really were. But there was nothing that I could do about it, so I opened my book to its center and began browsing through the spotted pages. Girls with blond braids and boys with blue eyes stared up at me. I found a story about a boy and his dog lost in a cave and began reading while Miss Crocker's voice droned on monotonously.

Suddenly I grew conscious of a break in that monotonous tone and I looked up. Miss Crocker was sitting at Miss Davis's desk with the first-grade books stacked before her, staring fiercely down at Little Man, who was pushing a book back upon the desk.

"What's that you said, Clayton Chester Logan?" she asked.

The room became gravely silent. Everyone knew that Little Man was in big trouble for no one, but no one, ever called Little Man "Clayton Chester" unless she or he meant serious business.

Little Man knew this too. His lips parted slightly as he took his hands from the book. He quivered, but he did not take his eyes from Miss Crocker. "I—I said may I have another book please, ma'am," he squeaked. "That one's dirty."

"Dirty!" Miss Crocker echoed, appalled by such temerity.[4] She stood up, gazing down upon Little Man like a bony giant, but Little Man raised his head and continued to look into her eyes. "Dirty! And just who do you think you are, Clayton Chester? Here the county is giving us these wonderful books during these hard times and you're going to stand there and tell me that the book's too dirty? Now you take that book or get nothing at all!"

Little Man lowered his eyes and said nothing as he stared at the book. For several moments he stood there, his face barely visible above the desk, then he turned and looked at the few remaining books and, seeming to realize that they were as badly soiled as the one Miss Crocker had given him, he looked across the room at me. I nodded and Little Man, glancing up again at Miss Crocker, slid the book from the edge of the desk, and with his back straight and his head up returned to his seat.

Miss Crocker sat down again. "Some people around here seem to be giving themselves airs. I'll tolerate no

---

3. **penchant**: desire.
4. **temerity**: rudeness; boldness.

more of that," she scowled. "Sharon Lake, come get your book."

I watched Little Man as he scooted into his seat beside two other little boys. He sat for a while with a stony face looking out the window; then, evidently accepting the fact that the book in front of him was the best that he could expect, he turned and opened it. But as he stared at the book's inside cover, his face clouded, changing from sulky acceptance to puzzlement. His brows furrowed. Then his eyes grew wide, and suddenly he sucked in his breath and sprang from his chair like a wounded animal, flinging the book onto the floor and stomping madly upon it.

Miss Crocker rushed to Little Man and grabbed him up in powerful hands. She shook him vigorously, then set him on the floor again. "Now, just what's gotten into you, Clayton Chester?"

But Little Man said nothing. He just stood staring down at the open book, shivering with indignant anger.

"Pick it up," she ordered.

"No!" defied Little Man.

"No? I'll give you ten seconds to pick up that book, boy, or I'm going to get my switch."

Little Man bit his lower lip, and I knew that he was not going to pick up the book. Rapidly, I turned to the inside cover of my own book and saw immediately what had made Little Man so furious. Stamped on the inside cover was a chart which read:

	PROPERTY OF THE BOARD OF EDUCATION		
	Spokane County, Mississippi September, 1922		
Chronological Issuance	Date of Issuance	Condition of Book	Race of Student
1	September 1922	New	White
2	September 1923	Excellent	White
3	September 1924	Excellent	White
4	September 1925	Very Good	White
5	September 1926	Good	White
6	September 1927	Good	White
7	September 1928	Average	White
8	September 1929	Average	White
9	September 1930	Average	White
10	September 1931	Poor	White
11	September 1932	Poor	White
12	September 1933	Very Poor	nigra
13			
14			
15			

The blank lines continued down to line 20 and I knew that they had all been reserved for black students. A knot of anger swelled in my throat and held there. But as Miss Crocker directed Little Man to bend over the "whipping" chair, I put aside my anger and jumped up.

"Miz Crocker, don't, please!" I cried. Miss Crocker's dark eyes warned me not to say another word. "I know why he done it!"

"You want part of this switch, Cassie?"

"No'm," I said hastily. "I just wanna tell you how come Little Man done what he done."

"Sit down!" she ordered as I hurried toward her with the open book in my hand.

Holding the book up to her, I said, "See, Miz Crocker, see what it says. They give us these ole books when they didn't want 'em no more."

She regarded me impatiently, but did not look at the book. "Now how could he know what it says? He can't read."

"Yes'm, he can. He been reading since he was four. He can't read all them big words, but he can read them columns. See what's in the last row. Please look, Miz Crocker."

This time Miss Crocker did look, but her face did not change. Then, holding up her head, she gazed unblinkingly down at me.

"S-see what they called us," I said, afraid she had not seen.

"That's what you are," she said coldly. "Now go sit down."

I shook my head, realizing now that Miss Crocker did not even know what I was talking about. She had looked at the page and had understood nothing.

"I said sit down, Cassie!"

I started slowly toward my desk, but as the hickory stick sliced the tense air, I turned back around. "Miz Crocker," I said, "I don't want my book neither."

The switch landed hard upon Little Man's upturned bottom. Miss Crocker looked questioningly at me as I reached up to her desk and placed the book upon it. Then she swung the switch five more times and, discovering that Little Man had no intention of crying, ordered him up.

"All right, Cassie," she sighed, turning to me, "come on and get yours."

By the end of the school day I had decided that I would tell Mama everything before Miss Crocker had a chance to do so. From nine years of trial and error, I had learned that punishment was always less severe when I poured out the whole truth to Mama on my own before she had heard anything from anyone else. I knew that Miss Crocker had not spoken to Mama during the lunch period, for she had spent the whole hour in the classroom preparing for the afternoon session.

As soon as class was dismissed I sped from the room, weaving a path through throngs of students happy to be free. But before I could reach the seventh-grade-class building, I had the misfortune to collide with Mary Lou's father. Mr. Wellever looked down on me with surprise that I would actually bump into him, then proceeded to lecture me on the virtues of watching where one was going. Meanwhile Miss Crocker briskly crossed the lawn to

Mama's class building. By the time I escaped Mr. Wellever, she had already disappeared into the darkness of the hallway.

Mama's classroom was in the back. I crept silently along the quiet hall and peeped cautiously into the open doorway. Mama, pushing a strand of her long, crinkly hair back into the chignon at the base of her slender neck, was seated at her desk watching Miss Crocker thrust a book before her. "Just look at that, Mary," Miss Crocker said, thumping the book twice with her forefinger. "A perfectly good book ruined. Look at that broken binding and those foot marks all over it."

Mama did not speak as she studied the book.

"And here's the one Cassie wouldn't take," she said, placing a second book on Mama's desk with an outraged slam. "At least she didn't have a tantrum and stomp all over hers. I tell you, Mary, I just don't know what got into those children today. I always knew Cassie was rather high-strung, but Little Man! He's always such a perfect little gentleman."

Mama glanced at the book I had rejected and opened the front cover so that the offensive pages of both books faced her. "You say Cassie said it was because of this front page that she and Little Man didn't want the books?" Mama asked quietly.

"Yes, ain't that something?" Miss Crocker said, forgetting her teacher-training-school diction in her indignation. "The very idea! That's on all the books, and why they got so upset about it I'll never know."

"You punish them?" asked Mama, glancing up at Miss Crocker.

"Well, I certainly did! Whipped both of them good with my hickory stick. Wouldn't you have?" When Mama did not reply, she added defensively, "I had a perfect right to."

"Of course you did, Daisy," Mama said, turning back to the books again. "They disobeyed you." But her tone was so quiet and noncommittal[5] that I knew Miss Crocker was not satisfied with her reaction.

"Well, I thought you would've wanted to know, Mary, in case you wanted to give them a piece of your mind also."

Mama smiled up at Miss Crocker and said rather absently, "Yes, of course, Daisy. Thank you." Then she opened her desk drawer and pulled out some paper, a pair of scissors, and a small brown bottle.

Miss Crocker, dismayed by Mama's seeming unconcern for the seriousness of the matter, thrust her shoulders back and began moving away from the desk. "You understand that if they don't have those books to study from, I'll have to fail them in both reading and composition, since I plan to base all my lessons around—" She stopped abruptly and stared in amazement at Mama. "Mary, what in the world are you doing?"

Mama did not answer. She had trimmed the paper to the size of the books and was now dipping a gray-looking glue from the brown bottle onto the inside cover of one of the books. Then she took the paper and placed it over the glue.

"Mary Logan, do you know what you're doing? That book belongs to the county. If somebody from the superintendent's office ever comes down here and sees that book, you'll be in real trouble."

Mama laughed and picked up the other book. "In the first place no one cares enough to come down here, and in the second place if anyone should come, maybe he could see all the things we need—current books for all of our subjects, not just somebody's old throwaways, desks, paper, blackboards, erasers, maps, chalk..." Her voice trailed off as she glued the second book.

"Biting the hand that feeds you. That's what you're doing, Mary Logan, biting the hand that feeds you."

Again, Mama laughed. "If that's the case, Daisy, I don't think I need that little bit of food." With the second book finished, she stared at a small pile of seventh-grade books on her desk.

"Well, I just think you're spoiling those children, Mary. They've got to learn how things are sometime."

"Maybe so," said Mama, "but that doesn't mean they have to accept them ...and maybe we don't either."

Miss Crocker gazed suspiciously at Mama. Although Mama had been a teacher at Great Faith for fourteen years, ever since she had graduated from the Crandon Teacher Training School at nineteen, she was still considered by many of the other teachers as a disrupting maverick. Her ideas were always a bit too radical and

---

5. **noncommittal:** without opinion.

her statements a bit too pointed. The fact that she had not grown up in Spokane County but in the Delta made her even more suspect, and the more traditional thinkers like Miss Crocker were wary of her. "Well, if anyone ever does come from the county and sees Cassie's and Little Man's books messed up like that," she said, "I certainly won't accept the responsibility for them."

"It will be easy enough for anyone to see whose responsibility it is, Daisy, by opening any seventh-grade book. Because tomorrow I'm going to 'mess them up' too."

Miss Crocker, finding nothing else to say, turned imperiously and headed for the door. I dashed across the hall and awaited her exit, then crept back.

Mama remained at her desk, sitting very still. For a long time she did not move. When she did, she picked up one of the seventh-grade books and began to glue again. I wanted to go and help her, but something warned me that now was not the time to make my presence known, and I left.

I would wait until the evening to talk to her; there was no rush now. She understood.

*George Orwell often expressed his political opinions in his writing. In his novel **Animal Farm**, published in 1945, he wrote about the dangers of a totalitarian government. You will get a good sense of how Orwell feels about this type of government by studying the actions of the characters in this excerpt from **Animal Farm**. The characters are farm animals that act like people.*

This excerpt begins with Chapter 2 the day after the animals rebel against Jones, the farmer who owns them. They chase him and his wife off the farm and set up a new government. The animals include three pigs: Snowball, Napoleon, and Squealer; the horses: Boxer, Clover, and Mollie; the donkey Old Benjamin; the cat; and various other barnyard animals. Read carefully to see how the animals set up a new government, and predict if each animal will be treated equally.

From

Animal Farm

George Orwell (1903–1950)

The animals had their breakfast, and then Snowball and Napoleon called them together again.

"Comrades," said Snowball, "it is half-past six and we have a long day before us. Today we begin the hay harvest. But there is another matter that must be attended to first."

The pigs now revealed that during the past three months they had taught themselves to read and write from an old spelling book which had belonged to Mr. Jones's children and which had been thrown on the rubbish heap. Napoleon sent for pots of black and white paint and led the way down to the five-barred gate that gave on to the main road. Then Snowball (for it was Snowball who was best at writing) took a brush between the two knuckles of his trotter, painted out MANOR

FARM from the top bar of the gate and in its place painted ANIMAL FARM. This was to be the name of the farm from now onwards. After this they went back to the farm buildings, where Snowball and Napoleon sent for a ladder which they caused to be set against the end wall of the big barn. They explained that by their studies of the past three months the pigs had succeeded in reducing the principles of Animalism to Seven Commandments. These Seven Commandments would now be inscribed on the wall; they would form an unalterable law by which all the animals on Animal Farm must live for ever after. With some difficulty (for it is not easy for a pig to balance himself on a ladder) Snowball climbed up and set to work, with Squealer a few rungs below him holding the paint-pot. The Commandments were written on the tarred wall in great white letters that could be read thirty yards away. They ran thus:

THE SEVEN COMMANDMENTS

1. *Whatever goes upon two legs is an enemy.*

2. *Whatever goes upon four legs, or has wings, is a friend.*

3. *No animal shall wear clothes.*

4. *No animal shall sleep in a bed.*

5. *No animal shall drink alcohol.*

6. *No animal shall kill any other animal.*

7. *All animals are equal.*

It was very neatly written, and except that "friend" was written "freind" and one of the "S's" was the wrong way round, the spelling was correct all the way through. Snowball read it aloud for the benefit of the others. All the animals nodded in complete agreement, and the cleverer ones at once began to learn the Commandments by heart.

"Now, comrades," cried Snowball, throwing down the paint-brush, "to the hayfield! Let us make it a point of honour to get in the harvest more quickly than Jones and his men could do."

But at this moment the three cows, who had seemed uneasy for some time past, set up a loud lowing. They had not been milked for twenty-four hours, and their udders were almost bursting. After a little thought, the pigs sent for buckets and milked the cows fairly successfully, their trotters being well adapted to this task. Soon there were five buckets of frothing creamy milk at which many of the animals looked with considerable interest.

"What is going to happen to all that milk?" said someone.

"Jones used sometimes to mix some of it in our mash," said one of the hens.

"Never mind the milk, comrades!" cried Napoleon, placing himself in front of the buckets. "That will be attended to. The harvest is more important. Comrade Snowball will lead the way. I shall follow in a few minutes. Forward, comrades! The hay is waiting."

So the animals trooped down to the hayfield to begin the harvest, and when they came back in the evening it was noticed that the milk had disappeared.

Chapter 3

How they toiled and sweated to get the hay in! But their efforts were rewarded, for the harvest was an even bigger success than they had hoped.

Sometimes the work was hard; the implements had been designed for human beings and not for animals, and it was a great drawback that no animal was able to use any tool that involved standing on his hind legs. But the pigs were so clever that they could think of a way round every difficulty. As for the horses, they knew every inch of the field, and in fact understood the business of mowing and raking far better than Jones and his men had ever done. The pigs did not actually work, but directed and supervised the others. With their superior knowledge it was natural that they should assume the leadership. Boxer and Clover would harness themselves to the cutter or the horse-rake (no bits or reins were needed in these days, of course) and tramp steadily round and round the field with a pig walking behind and calling out "Gee up, comrade!" or "Whoa back, comrade!" as the case might be. And every animal down to the humblest worked at turning the hay and gathering it. Even the ducks and hens toiled to and fro all day in the sun, carrying tiny wisps of hay in their beaks. In the end they finished the harvest in two days' less time than it had usually taken Jones and his men. Moreover, it was the biggest harvest that the farm had ever seen. There was no wastage whatever; the hens and ducks with their sharp eyes had gathered up the very last stalk. And not an animal on the farm had stolen so much as a mouthful.

All through that summer the work of the farm went like clockwork. The animals were happy as they had never conceived it possible to be. Every mouthful of food was an acute positive pleasure, now that it was truly their own food, produced by themselves and for themselves, not doled out to them by a grudging master. With the worthless parasitical human beings gone, there was more for everyone to eat. There was more leisure too, inexperienced though the animals were. They met with many difficulties—for instance, later in the year, when they harvested the corn, they had to tread it out in the ancient style and blow away the chaff with their breath, since the farm possessed no threshing machine—but the pigs with their cleverness and Boxer with his tremendous muscles always pulled them through. Boxer was the admiration of everybody. He had been a hard worker even in Jones's time, but now he seemed more like three horses than one; there were days when the entire work of the farm seemed to rest on his mighty shoulders. From morning to night he was pushing and pulling, always at the spot where the work was hardest. He had made an arrangement with one of the cockerels to call him in the mornings half an hour earlier than anyone else, and would put in some volunteer labour at whatever seemed to be most needed, before the regular day's work began. His answer to every problem, every setback, was "I will work harder!"—which he had adopted as his personal motto.

But everyone worked according to his capacity. The hens and ducks, for instance, saved five bushels of corn at each harvest by gathering up the stray grains. Nobody stole, nobody grumbled over his rations, the quarrelling and biting and jealousy which had been normal features of life in the old days had almost disappeared. Nobody shirked¹—or almost nobody. Mollie, it was true, was not good at getting up in the mornings, and had a way of leaving work early on the ground that there was a stone in her hoof. And the behaviour of the cat was somewhat peculiar. It was soon noticed that when there was work to be done the cat could never be found. She would vanish for hours on end, and then reappear at meal-times, or in the evening after work was over, as though nothing had happened. But she always made such excellent excuses, and purred so affectionately, that it was impossible not to believe in her good intentions. Old Benjamin, the donkey, seemed quite unchanged since the Rebellion. He did his work in the same slow obstinate way as he had done it in Jones's time, never shirking and never volunteering for extra work either. About the Rebellion and its results he would express no opinion. When asked

whether he was not happier now that Jones was gone, he would say only, "Donkeys live a long time. None of you has ever seen a dead donkey," and the others had to be content with this cryptic answer.

On Sundays there was no work. Breakfast was an hour later than usual, and after breakfast there was a ceremony which was observed every week without fail. First came the hoisting of the flag. Snowball had found in the harness-room an old green tablecloth of Mrs. Jones's and had painted on it a hoof and a horn in white. This was run up the flagstaff in the farmhouse garden every Sunday morning. The flag was green, Snowball

---

1. **shirked:** avoided work.

explained, to represent the green fields of England, while the hoof and horn signified the future Republic of the Animals which would arise when the human race had been finally overthrown. After the hoisting of the flag all the animals trooped into the big barn for a general assembly which was known as the Meeting. Here the work of the coming week was planned out and resolutions[2] were put forward and debated. It was always the pigs who put forward the resolutions. The other animals understood how to vote, but could never think of any resolutions of their own. Snowball and Napoleon were by far the most active in the debates. But it was noticed that these two were never in agreement: whatever suggestion either of them made, the other could be counted on to oppose it. Even when it was resolved—a thing no one could object to in itself—to set aside the small paddock behind the orchard as a home of rest for animals who were past work, there was a stormy debate over the correct retiring age for each class of animal. The Meeting always ended with the singing of *Beasts of England,* and the afternoon was given up to recreation.

The pigs had set aside the harness-room as a headquarters for themselves. Here, in the evenings, they studied blacksmithing, carpentering, and other necessary arts from books which they had brought out of the farmhouse. Snowball also busied himself with organising the other animals into what he called Animal Committees. He was indefatigable[3] at this. He formed the Egg Production Committee for the hens, the Clean Tails League for the cows, the Wild Comrades' Re-education Committee (the object of this was to tame the rats and rabbits), the Whiter Wool Movement for the sheep, and various others, besides instituting classes in reading and writing. On the whole, these projects were a failure. The attempt to tame the wild creatures, for instance, broke down almost immediately. They continued to behave very much as before, and when treated with generosity, simply took advantage of it. The cat joined the Re-education Committee and was very active in it for some days. She was seen one day sitting on a roof and talking to some sparrows who were just out of her reach. She was telling them that all the animals were now comrades and that any sparrow who chose could come and perch on her paw; but the sparrows kept their distance.

The reading and writing classes, however, were a great success. By the autumn almost every animal on the farm was literate in some degree.

As for the pigs, they could already read and write perfectly. The dogs learned to read fairly well, but were not interested in reading anything except the Seven Commandments. Muriel, the goat, could read somewhat better than the dogs, and sometimes used to read to the others in the evenings from scraps of newspaper which she found on the rubbish heap. Benjamin could

---

2. **resolutions:** courses of action.
3. **indefatigable:** never tired; full of energy.

then decorate them with a flower or two and walk round them admiring them.

None of the other animals on the farm could get further than the letter A. It was also found that the stupider animals, such as the sheep, hens, and ducks, were unable to learn the Seven Commandments by heart. After much thought Snowball declared that the Seven Commandments could in effect be reduced to a single maxim,[4] namely: "Four legs good, two legs bad." This, he said, contained the essential principle of Animalism. Whoever had thoroughly grasped it would be safe from human influences. The birds at first objected, since it seemed to them that they also had two legs, but Snowball proved to them that this was not so.

"A bird's wing, comrades," he said, "is an organ of propulsion and not of manipulation. It should therefore be regarded as a leg. The distinguishing mark of man is the *hand,* the instrument with which he does all his mischief."

The birds did not understand Snowball's long words, but they accepted his explanation, and all the humbler animals set to work to learn the new maxim by heart. FOUR LEGS GOOD, TWO LEGS BAD, was inscribed on the end wall of the barn, above the Seven Commandments and in bigger letters. When they had once got it by heart, the sheep developed a great liking for this maxim, and often

read as well as any pig, but never exercised his faculty. So far as he knew, he said, there was nothing worth reading. Clover learnt the whole alphabet, but could not put words together. Boxer could not get beyond the letter D. He would trace out A, B, C, D, in the dust with his great hoof, and then would stand staring at the letters with his ears back, sometimes shaking his forelock, trying with all his might to remember what came next and never succeeding. On several occasions, indeed, he did learn E, F, G, H, but by the time he knew them, it was always discovered that he had forgotten A, B, C, and D. Finally he decided to be content with the first four letters, and used to write them out once or twice every day to refresh his memory. Mollie refused to learn any but the six letters which spelt her own name. She would form these very neatly out of pieces of twig, and would

---

4. **maxim:** saying.

as they lay in the field they would all start bleating "Four legs good, two legs bad! Four legs good, two legs bad!" and keep it up for hours on end, never growing tired of it.

Napoleon took no interest in Snowball's committees. He said that the education of the young was more important than anything that could be done for those who were already grown up. It happened that Jessie and Bluebell had both whelped soon after the hay harvest, giving birth between them to nine sturdy puppies. As soon as they were weaned, Napoleon took them away from their mothers, saying that he would make himself responsible for their education. He took them up into a loft which could only be reached by a ladder from the harness-room, and there kept them in such seclusion that the rest of the farm soon forgot their existence.

The mystery of where the milk went to was soon cleared up. It was mixed every day into the pigs' mash. The early apples were now ripening, and the grass of the orchard was littered with windfalls. The animals had assumed as a matter of course that these would be shared out equally; one day, however, the order went forth that all windfalls were to be collected and brought to the harness-room for the use of the pigs. At this some of the other animals murmured, but it was no use. All the pigs were in full agreement on this point, even Snowball and Napoleon. Squealer was sent to make the necessary explanations to the others.

"Comrades!" he cried. "You do not imagine, I hope, that we pigs are doing this in a spirit of selfishness and privilege? Many of us actually dislike milk and apples. I dislike them myself. Our sole object in taking these things is to preserve our health. Milk and apples (this has been proved by Science, comrades) contain substances absolutely necessary to the well-being of a pig. We pigs are brainworkers. The whole management and organisation of this farm depend on us. Day and night we are watching over your welfare. It is for *your* sake that we drink that milk and eat those apples. Do you know what would happen if we pigs failed in our duty? Jones would come back! Yes, Jones would come back! Surely, comrades," cried Squealer almost pleadingly, skipping from side to side and whisking his tail, "surely there is no one among you who wants to see Jones come back?"

Now if there was one thing that the animals were completely certain of, it was that they did not want Jones back. When it was put to them in this light, they had no more to say. The importance of keeping the pigs in good health was all too obvious. So it was agreed without further argument that the milk and the windfall apples (and also the main crop of apples when they ripened) should be reserved for the pigs alone.

Unit 3: Nonfiction

One writes to make a home for oneself,
on paper, in time and in others' minds.
Alfred Kazin

In the first two units of this anthology, you were introduced to fiction, which is literature that is not true. In this unit, you will read nonfiction. Keep in mind that nonfiction is true.

In two of the nonfiction selections, the authors recall events in their own lives. One author writes about her memories as a Japanese-American during World War II. Another author takes you to Africa as she shares the joy of helping others. As you read each selection, pay special attention to how the writer reacts to her experiences.

In addition to reading about people's lives, you will read about their opinions. One author will amuse you with her humorous outlook on diets. Another author takes a look at soap operas. At first, you may think her commentary contains only facts. A closer look will reveal her opinions—which you may accept or reject. As you read each selection, think about the writer's purpose. Is her purpose to inform you, entertain you, or persuade you?

Although nonfiction is true, you will find it is as much fun and sometimes more amazing than stories that are imaginary. You may even want to try your own hand at writing nonfiction!

*This informal essay comes from Kerr's book **How I Got to Be Perfect**, in which she focuses on life as a woman. As you read, enjoy the light-heartedness of this essay, and ask yourself why Kerr uses humor to express her ideas.*

My Marshmallow Fudge Wonder Diet

Jean Kerr (1923–   )

Fred Allen used to talk about a man who was so thin he could be dropped through a piccolo[1] without striking a single note. Well, I'm glad I never met *him*; I'd hate to have to hear about *his* diet.

I can remember when I was a girl—way back in Truman's administration—and Tab was only a gleam in the eye of the Coca-Cola Bottling Company. In those days it was fun to go to parties. The conversation used to crackle with wit and intelligence because we talked about *ideas*—the aesthetic continuum in Western culture, Gary Cooper in western movies, the superiority of beer over lotion as a wave-set, and the best way to use leftover veal.

Go to a party now and the couple next to you won't say a word about the rich, chocolate texture of their compost heap or how practical it's been to buy bunk beds for the twins. They won't talk about anything whatsoever except their diets—the one they've just come off, the one they're on now, or the one they're going to have to start on Monday if they keep lapping it up like this.

I really blame science for the whole business. Years ago when a man began to notice that if he stood up on the subway and he was immediately replaced by *two* people, he figured he

---

1. piccolo: a small flute.

was getting too fat. So he went to his doctor and the doctor said, "Quit stuffing yourself, Joe." And Joe either stopped or he didn't stop, but at least he kept his big mouth shut about the whole matter. What was there to talk about?

Today, with the science of nutrition advancing so rapidly, there is plenty of food for conversation, if for nothing else. We have Dr. Stillman's "Water Diet," Dr. Frank's "No Aging Diet" in which every cell in your body becomes young as a result of your consumption of sardines and lentils, Dr. Rubin's "Save Your Life Diet" in which you duplicate the eating habits of the developing African nations (fibers, you

eat more fibers), Dr. Jollife's "The Prudent Diet," Dr. Atkins' "The Super Energy Diet," and finally Dr. Linn's "The Last Chance Diet" in which you don't eat anything whatsoever except two tablespoons of a cherry-flavored potion call Prolinn. (It's called other things by people who have to swallow it.)

But where do people come across all these crazy diets, anyway? Obviously in the magazines; it's impossible to get a diet from a newspaper. For one thing, in a newspaper you can never catch the diet when it *starts*. It's always the fourth day of "Ada May's Wonder Diet" and, after a brief description of a simple slimming

My Marshmallow Fudge Wonder Diet   **59**

exercise that could be performed by anybody who has had five years' training with the ballet, Ada May gives you the menu for the day. One glass of skim milk, eight prunes, and three lamb kidneys. This settles the matter for most people, who figure, quite reasonably, that if this is the *fourth* day, heaven deliver them from the first.

However, any stoics[2] in the group who want to know just how far Ada May's sense of whimsy will take her can have the complete diet by sending sixty-two cents in stamps to the newspaper. But there you are. Who has sixty-two cents in stamps? You're not running a branch of the post office. And if you're going to go out and get the stamps you might as well buy a magazine which will give you not only the same diet (now referred to as "*Our Wonder Diet*") but will, in addition, show you a quick and easy way to turn your husband's old socks into gay pot holders.

In a truly democratic magazine that looks at all sides of the picture you will also find a recipe for George Washington's favorite spice cake, which will replace any weight you may have haphazardly lost on that wonder diet.

And where is all this dieting getting us? No place at all. It's taken all the fun out of conversation and all the joy out of cooking. Furthermore, it leads to acts of irrational violence. A friend of mine keeps all candy and other luscious tidbits in the freezer, on the theory that by the time they thaw out enough to be eaten she will have recovered her will

power. But the other night, having been driven berserk by a four-color advertisement for Instant Brownies, she rushed out to the freezer, started to gnaw on a frozen Milky Way, and broke off her front tooth.

But let's get to the heart of the matter. All these diets that appear so monotonously in the flossy magazines—who are they for? Are they aimed at men? Certainly not; most men don't read these magazines. Are they intended for fat teen-agers? Probably not; teen-agers can't afford them. Do not ask for whom the bell tolls. It tolls for you, Married Woman, Mother of Three, lumpy, dumpy, and the source of concern to practically every publication in the country. And why, why is the married woman being hounded into starvation in order to duplicate an ideal figure which is neither practical nor possible for a person her age? I'll tell you why.

First, it is presumed that when you're thinner you live longer. Those people in the Russian Ukraine who eat so much yogurt apparently live to be a hundred and thirty-four. (And when they have a cake with candles it must be something to see.) Second, it is felt that when you are skin and bones you have so much extra energy that you can climb up and shingle the roof. Third— and this is what they're really getting at—when you're thin you are so tasty and desirable that strange men will pinch you at the A & P and your husband will not only follow you around the kitchen breathing heavily

2. **stoics:** people not moved by pleasure or pain.

but will stop and smother you with kisses as you try to put the butter back in the icebox. This—and I hope those in the back of the room are listening—is hogwash.

Think of the happy marriages you know about. How many of the ladies are still wearing size twelve? I've been giving this a lot of thought in the last twenty minutes, and I have been examining the marriages in my own troubled circle. More than that, I have taken a cross section of the divorcees. (Cross? My dear, they were irate!) What I have discovered—attention, Beauty Editors everywhere!—is that women who are being ditched are one and all willowy, wandlike, and slim as a blade. In fact, six of them require extensive padding even to look flat-chested.

That the fourteen divorcees, or about-to-be divorcees, whom I happen to know personally are thin may be nothing more than a coincidence. Or it may just prove that men don't divorce fat wives because they feel sorry for them. Then again—and this is rather sinister—men may not divorce fat wives because they imagine that the poor, plump dears will never locate *another* husband and they'll be paying alimony to the end of their days. (I mention this possibility, but my heart's not in it.)

The real reason, I believe, that men hang onto their well-endowed spouses is because they're comfy and nice to have around the house. In a marriage there is nothing that stales so fast as physical beauty—as we readers of *Modern Screen* have observed. What actually holds a husband through thick and thick is a girl who is fun to be with. And any girl who has had nothing to eat since nine o'clock this morning but three hard-boiled eggs will be about as jolly and companionable as an income-tax inspector.

So I say, ladies, find out why women everywhere are switching from old-fashioned diets to the *modern* way: no exercise, no dangerous drugs, no weight loss. (And what do they mean "ugly fat"? It's *you* isn't it?) For that tired run-down feeling, try eating three full meals a day with a candy bar after dinner and pizza at eleven o'clock. Don't be intimidated by pictures of Farrah Fawcett-Majors. That girl simply has more teeth than other people. Just sit there smiling on that size twenty backside and say "Guess what we're having for dinner, dear? Your favorite—stuffed breast of veal and corn fritters." All of your friends will say "Oh, Blanche is a mess, the size of a house, but he's crazy about her, just *crazy* about her!"

As early as 1925, millions of people turned on their radios to listen to their favorite radio serials. Because soap companies sponsored these programs, they were called soap operas. With the invention of television in the 1950s, soap operas continued to attract a wide audience. Why are soap operas so popular? Read this commentary by Molly Ivins to find out what she thinks. Do you agree?

Daytime Soaps: The Best and the Brightest

Molly Ivins (1944–   )

Everybody likes to make fun of the soaps—everybody who doesn't watch them, that is. "Absurd," "silly" and "unrealistic" are the most common charges leveled against daytime drama. Nonsense. Donald Westlake, the novelist, has observed that fiction writers labor under the restraint of plausibility:[1] their inventions must stay within the capacity of the audience to accept and believe. God, of course, working with facts, faces no such limitation. Real life is far more improbable than soap operas. Will they ever get General Noriega out of Panama? Will Mary Beth Whitehead-Gould ever get that baby back? These and other real-life serials strain our credulity[2] daily; the front page is much weirder than *As the World Turns*.

College students and housewives, cleaning ladies and cops, teachers in the teachers' lounge and lawmakers in the cloakroom all watch the soaps. Economists worried about productivity might want to take a close look at how so many people with 9-to-5 jobs manage to follow the soaps. Those who consider soap operas an intellectual vacuum may want to ponder the fact that they're among the most popular

---

1. restraint of plausibility: limits of what seems probable.
2. credulity: readiness to believe.

programs on campus. A perfectly appalling number of the future leaders of our Nation cut class last year to watch Adrienne and Justin get married on NBC's *Days of Our Lives.*

So sink with us into the suds once more, as we examine the world where amnesia is more common than the cold and adultery more frequent than red lights. Anything can happen here, but one great certainty is that when one character desperately needs to reach another, that other will always have just left the room and the phone will ring...ring...ring.

Soap fans all have different favorites, but there's widespread agreement that CBS's *The Young and the Restless* is one of the best. *Y&R,* as the fan magazines call it, sticks with the strength of soaps—it's about people and their relationships. *The Young and the Restless* and CBS's *The Bold and the Beautiful* (both created by William J. Bell and Lee Phillip Bell) are technically better shows than most. While nothing on daytime television approaches the lush costumes and settings of the nighttime soaps, such as *Dallas* and *Dynasty, The Young and the Restless* comes closest. It's also the sexiest and the funniest of the daytime soaps.

It's possible that the worst of the soaps is ABC's *Loving,* a half-hour program that features a more exotic variety of unhappy love than even the most hardened soap fan can take. If, for example, character A is madly in love with character B and B should actually happen to return that regard, then, as sure as skunks stink, B will either die, turn out to be a Catholic priest with amnesia or to have both a previous life and a previous wife. While this is all pretty good stuff by soap standards, it comes in too concentrated a form on this show.

Several soaps are in the throes of spy and gangster plots, which require more than the usual suspension of disbelief. Suave dastards[3] wearing tuxes slink about swank nightclubs plotting crimes in a fashion never yet recorded on an FBI wiretap. Another trend that distresses many fans is the fantasy, where we suddenly dissolve into a character's daydream. It's not always clear this is happening. A character will drop to his knees and propose to the love of his life. Only after the next advertisement do we discover it was just her daydream. ABC's *One Life to Live* recently took fantasy a step further and plopped some of its characters into the Old West, not in a dream but a time warp. Even soap fans found it hard to believe.

The flashback is a happier innovation,[4] where brief scenes or snatches of dialogue from earlier shows are used to bring viewers up-to-date on what's been happening. Flashbacks can replace or supplement those endless soap scenes where two characters are having coffee and catching up: "Gosh, Jennifer, I haven't seen you since Eric told Stephanie he was leaving her for Tammy's daughter Melissa."

---

3. **suave dastards:** smooth villains.
4. **innovation:** new change.

"That's right, Julia. And that was even before Paige was killed in the automobile accident that gave Jason amnesia, so he can't remember who raped Marcy."

Part of the charm of soaps is that they leave a viewer in no doubt as to what emotion the drama is aiming for. If the dialogue doesn't give it away—"Frank, what will happen now??!!"—then the music will. There is mood music for suspense, for romance, for danger, for amazing news and for villainy afoot. These musical cues become so familiar, fans respond to them like Pavlov's dog.[5]

The grande dame[6] of all the conniving, scheming vixens who have ever graced the soaps is Erica Kane of ABC's *All My Children,* played by Susan Lucci. For 18 years, Erica has been manipulating and making trouble, so this year the show accorded her a special honor—an Erica retrospective. Her name was spelled out in big letters and her many, many ex-lovers and ex-husbands from years past came back to hash over old times. Erica has been a nasty bimbo for so long, fans have become quite fond of her, so her character is becoming more sympathetic: all she ever really wanted was love anyway. The new, more sympathetic Erica may not work; there are people who still haven't forgiven her for marrying that nice Jeff Martin and then breaking his heart. And that was quite some time ago.

The ditziest female on the soaps is Tina of *One Life to Live,* played by Andrea Evans. Tina is basically no good at being no good: she tries to manipulate others, but her stratagems are so transparent she hurts only herself. What Tina has in common with J.R. Ewing and other soap villains is that she never accepts a no. Rejection is not in this woman's vocabulary.

Tina has lately been the chief player in the finest bit of soap-opera plotting seen in years: the Baby Over the Waterfall caper. For reasons too complicated to explain, a very pregnant Tina was in South America when she was swept over a waterfall. A big one. Happily, she was rescued by primitive Indians who lived at the foot of the falls. She delivered her baby in their straw hut. They called the child Milagro. *But Tina didn't know she was a mother.* She thought she had lost the baby. Only when she got word of a blue-eyed baby in the jungle did the search for the child commence. The child was, of course, kidnapped by bad actors and taken to Venice and later stashed in a convent. The nuns lied and said the child wasn't there, so Tina infiltrated the convent disguised as "Sister Christina" and found her baby. Outstanding.

Good women on soaps, those clearly intended to be role models, are boring. Erica's mother is a saint, but a dreadful bore. Viki Buchanan of *One Life* is such a bore they had to give her a second personality to make her interesting.

---

5. **Pavlov's dog:** the dog that responds automatically in Pavlov's experiments.
6. **grande dame:** best example.

There's considerable division of opinion over who is the sexiest man on the soaps, but two leading contenders are both police chiefs—Roman Brady (Drake Hogestyn) of *Days of Our Lives* and Robert Scorpio (Tristan Rogers) of ABC's *General Hospital,* each with devoted fans. A young hunk on *The Bold and the Beautiful* is also attracting attention. Daniel McVicar plays a character who was brought in by a mother to woo her daughter. First he made a play for the mother, then the daughter's friend, before finally eloping with the daughter. Male villains are sometimes thugs, but more often dapper schemers like Sen. Harper Deveraux (Joseph Campanella) of *Days,* who was recently revealed to be the "Riverfront Slasher."

Soaps may not be high art, but they are socially useful. For one thing, they provide employment for an impressive number of actors who would otherwise be waiting tables. The soaps are a great place for actors before they go on to better things and for actors who have already done better things. Soap fans beam upon the genre's graduates proudly when they show up in prime time: "I remember Knight Rider when he was a divine young hunk on *The Young and the Restless!*"

All My Children is the most socially responsible of the soaps, always ready to tackle topical problems. The show's current treatment of AIDS is an excellent example of *AMC's* touch with touchy issues. Cindy Parker, who is played by Ellen Wheeler, contracts AIDS from her drug-addict husband. Cindy is a hairdresser and, in episodes about whether she should lose her job because of her illness, the show did an excellent job of presenting solid information about how AIDS is spread and whether it can be acquired through casual contact. It is possible to regard the soaps' treatment of topical issues as exploitation[7] of serious problems, but in fact the soaps are an excellent medium for popular education. *AMC* did not, however, make its AIDS patient a gay male. There are no gay males in daytime soaps yet.

Many soap conventions reflect the shows' earlier traditions. For example, most soaps are set in suburbs or small towns, even though many Americans live in cities now. In the days of the early radio soap operas—*Stella Dallas, Hilltop House,* and *Ma Perkins*—country people or hometown folks were always honest, simple and good, while city slickers were the con men and the smooth fellows who broke a girl's heart and left her crying.

As the soaps have become trendier, a new tolerance for those with unfortunate beginnings is manifest.[8] There are a remarkable number of ex-prostitutes now leading blameless lives on the soaps. The former hookers are quickly absorbed into the storyline and become temporarily blind or develop amnesia or sink into long comas right along with everyone else.

Ring...ring ...ring.

---

7. **exploitation:** taking advantage.
8. **manifest:** evident.

What would it be like if you couldn't read or write? In this excerpt from the book **Out of Africa,** *Isak Dinesen recalls when Jogona, a native who cannot read or write, asks her to record his story.*

After his friend Waweru died, Jogona cared for Waweru's wife and son Wamai. Jogona loved the child and thought of him as his own. One day, while several children were playing with a shotgun, Wamai was accidentally killed. The custom was to give the dead child's father a settlement, and Jogona was given 25 sheep. Soon after, three strangers appeared. They said that the sheep should be theirs because they were Wamai's uncles. Jogona asks the author to help him prove that the settlement for Wamai's death is rightfully his. Read to discover the results of Dinesen's willingness to help Jogona.

From

Out of Africa

Isak Dinesen (1885—1962)

But two days later Jogona came back early in the morning, when I was at my typewriter, and asked me to write down for him the account of his relations to the dead child and its family. He wanted to take the report before the D.C.[1] at Dagoretti. Jogona's very simple manner was impressive because he felt so strongly about things, and was entirely without self-consciousness. It was evident that he was looking upon his present resolution[2] as upon a great enterprise,[3] which was not without danger; he went to it with awe.

I wrote his statement down for him. It took a long time, for it was a long report of events more than six years old, and in themselves extremely

1. **D.C.:** District Commissioner.
2. **resolution:** course of action.
3. **enterprise:** project.

complicated. Jogona, as he was going through it, continually had to break off his tale to think things over or to go back in it and reconstruct it. He was, most of the time, holding his head with both hands, at moments gravely slapping the crown of it as if to shake out the facts. Once he went and leaned his face against the wall, as the Kikuyu[4] women do when they are giving birth to their children.

I took a duplicate of the report. I have still got it.

It was extremely difficult to follow, it gave a lot of complicated circumstances and irrelevant[5] details. It was not surprising to me that Jogona had found it difficult to recollect, it was more surprising that he should be able to recollect the facts at all. It began:

"At the time when Waweru Wamai, of Nyeri,[6] was about to die—*na-taka kufa,* wished to die, they have it in Swahili—he had two wives. The one wife had three daughters, after Waweru's death she married another man. The other wife, Waweru had not yet paid for altogether, he still owed her father two goats for her. This wife had overstrained herself when she lifted a load of firewood and had had a miscarriage and nobody knew if she would bear any more children. . . ."

It went on in this way, and dragged the reader into a thick maze of Kikuyu conditions and relations:

"This wife had one small child by the name of Wamai. At that same time he was sick, and the people believed that he had got small-pox. Waweru was

Edward N. Wilson; MINORITY MAN NO. 1; wood sculpture; 1958; 38" x8½" x8½"; State University of New York—Binghamton; University Art Museum Permanent Collection

very fond of his wife and of her child, and when he was dying he was very much worried because he did not know what would become of her when he himself should be dead. He therefore sent for his friend Jogona Kanyagga, who lived not far away. Jogona Kanyagga owed Waweru, at this time, three shillings for a pair of shoes. Waweru now suggested to him that they should make an agreement. . . ."

4. **Kikuyu:** the largest ethnic group in Kenya.
5. **irrelevant:** unrelated; unnecessary.
6. **Nyeri:** town in south central Kenya.

The agreement came to this that Jogona should take over his dying friend's wife and child, and pay to her father the two goats that were still due to him from the sum of her purchase price. From now the report became a list of expenses, which Jogona had brought upon himself through the adoption of the child Wamai. He had, he stated, purchased an extraordinary good medicine for Wamai just after he had taken him over, when he was sick. At some time he had bought rice from the Indian duca for him, as he did not thrive on maize.[7] Upon one occasion he had had to pay five Rupees to a white farmer of the neighbourhood, who said that Wamai had chased one of his turkeys into a pond. This last amount of hard cash, which he had probably had difficulty in raising, had stamped itself upon the mind of Jogona; he came back to it more than once. From Jogona's manner it appeared that he had, by this time, forgotten that the child whom he had now lost had not been his own. He was shaken by the arrival and the claim of the three Nyeri people, in many ways. Very simple people seem to have a talent for adopting children, and feeling towards them as if they were their own; the facile hearts of the European peasants do the same without effort.

When Jogona had at last come to the end of his tale, and I had got it all down, I told him that I was now going to read it to him. He turned away from me while I was reading, as if to avoid all distractions.

But as I read out his own name, "And he sent for Jogona Kanyagga, who was his friend and who lived not far away," he swiftly turned his face to me, and gave me a great fierce flaming glance, so exuberant with laughter that it changed the old man into a boy, into the very symbol of youth. Again as I had finished the document and was reading out his name, where it figured as a verification[8] below his thumb-mark, the vital direct glance was repeated, this time deepened and calmed, with a new dignity.

Such a glance did Adam give the Lord when He formed him out of the dust, and breathed into his nostrils the breath of life, and man became a living soul. I had created him and shown him himself: Jogona Kanyagga of life everlasting. When I handed him the paper, he took it reverently and greedily, folded it up in a corner of his cloak and kept his hand upon it. He could not afford to lose it, for his soul was in it, and it was the proof of his existence. Here was something which Jogona Kanyagga had performed, and which would preserve his name for ever: the flesh was made word and dwelt among us full of grace and truth.

As to Jogona's statement which I took down, it proved very useful to him, for when the D.C. had read it, he dismissed the appeal of the Nyeri people, who walked scowling back to their own village, without having got anything off the farm.

---

7. **maize:** corn.
8. **verification:** proof.

Aaron Douglas; THE CREATION; 1935; Permanent Collection; Howard University; Washington, D.C.

The document now became Jogona's great treasure. I saw it again more than once. Jogona made a little leather bag for it, embroidered with beads, and hung it on a strap round his neck. From time to time, mostly on Sunday mornings, he would suddenly appear in my door, lift the bag off and take out the paper to have it read to him. Once when I had been ill, and was for the first time again out riding, he caught sight of me at a distance, ran after me a long way, and stood by my horse all out of breath, to hand me his document. At each reading his face took on the same impress of deep religious triumph, and after the reading he solicitously smoothed out his paper, folded it up and put it back in the bag. The importance of the account was not lessened but augmented[9] with time, as if to Jogona the greatest wonder about it was that it did not change. The past, that had been so difficult to bring to memory, and that had probably seemed to be changing every time it was thought of, had here been caught, conquered and pinned down before his eyes. It had become History; with it there was now no variableness[10] neither shadow of turning.

9. **augmented**: increased.
10. **variableness**: change.

*The Japanese surprise attack on Pearl Harbor, December 7, 1941,
plunged the United States into World War II. A panic followed.
Almost all Japanese, even those who were American citizens,
were thought to be enemies. President Franklin D. Roosevelt
ordered them removed to camps far away from military
installations.*

*In this excerpt from **Farewell to Manzanar,** you will see through
a child's eyes how her mother struggles to keep the family
together after the father has been sent to a camp in North Dakota.
Read to find out how the child Jeanne feels when her life is turned
upside-down.*

From

Farewell to Manzanar

Jeanne Wakatsuki Houston (1934–)
and James D. Houston (1933–)

Chapter 2

Shikata Ga Nai

In December of 1941 Papa's disappearance didn't bother me nearly so much as the world I soon found myself in.

He had been a jack-of-all-trades. When I was born he was farming near Inglewood. Later, when he started fishing, we moved to Ocean Park, near Santa Monica, and until they picked him up, that's where we lived, in a big frame house with a brick fireplace, a block back from the beach. We were the only Japanese family in the neighborhood. Papa liked it that way. He didn't want to be labeled or grouped by anyone. But with him gone and no way of knowing what to expect, my mother moved all of us down to Terminal Island. Woody already lived there, and one of my older sisters had married a Terminal Island boy.

Mama's first concern now was to keep the family together; and once the war began, she felt safer there than isolated racially in Ocean Park. But for me, at age seven, the island was a country as foreign as India or Arabia would have been. It was the first time I had lived among other Japanese, or gone to school with them, and I was terrified all the time.

This was partly Papa's fault. One of his threats to keep us younger kids in line was "I'm going to sell you to the Chinaman." When I had entered kindergarten two years earlier, I was the only Oriental in the class. They sat me next to a Caucasian girl who happened to have very slanted eyes. I looked at her and began to scream, certain Papa had sold me out at last. My fear of her ran so deep I could not speak of it, even to Mama, couldn't explain why I was screaming. For two weeks I had nightmares about this girl, until the teachers finally moved me to the other side of the room. And it was still with me, this fear of Oriental faces, when we moved to Terminal Island.

In those days it was a company town, a ghetto owned and controlled by the canneries. The men went after fish, and whenever the boats came back—day or night—the women would be called to process the catch while it was fresh. One in the afternoon or four in the morning, it made no difference. My mother had to go to work right after we moved there. I can still hear the whistle—two toots for French's, three for Van Camp's—and she and Chizu would be out of bed in the middle of the night, heading for the cannery.

The house we lived in was nothing more than a shack, a barracks with single plank walls and rough wooden floors, like the cheapest kind of migrant workers' housing. The people around us were hardworking, boisterous,[1] a little proud of their nickname, *yo-go-re,* which meant literally *uncouth*[2] *one,* or roughneck, or dead-end kid. They not only spoke Japanese exclusively, they spoke a dialect peculiar to Kyushu, where their families had come from in Japan, a rough, fisherman's language, full of oaths and insults. Instead of saying *ba-ka-ta-re,* a common insult meaning *stupid,* Terminal Islanders would say *ba-ka-ya-ro,* a coarser and exclusively masculine use of the word, which implies gross stupidity. They would swagger and pick on outsiders and persecute anyone who didn't speak as they did. That was what made my own time there so hateful. I had never spoken anything but English, and the other kids in the second grade despised me for it. They were tough and mean, like ghetto kids anywhere. Each day after school I dreaded their ambush. My brother Kiyo, three years older, would wait for me at the door, where we would decide whether to run straight home together, or split up, or try a new and unexpected route.

None of these kids ever actually attacked. It was the threat that frightened us, their fearful looks, and the noises they would make, like

---

1. **boisterous:** loud.
2. **uncouth:** crude.

miniature Samurai,[3] in a language we couldn't understand.

At the time it seemed we had been living under this reign of fear for years. In fact, we lived there about two months. Late in February the navy decided to clear Terminal Island completely. Even though most of us were American-born, it was dangerous having that many Orientals so close to the Long Beach Naval Station, on the opposite end of the island. We had known something like this was coming. But, like Papa's arrest, not much could be done ahead of time. There were four of us kids still young enough to be living with Mama, plus Granny, her mother, sixty-five then, speaking no English, and nearly blind. Mama didn't know where else she could get work, and we had nowhere else to move *to*. On February 25 the choice was made for us. We were given forty-eight hours to clear out.

The secondhand dealers had been prowling around for weeks, like wolves, offering humiliating prices for goods and furniture they knew many of us would have to sell sooner or later. Mama had left all but her most valuable possessions in Ocean Park, simply because she had nowhere to put them. She had brought along her pottery, her silver, heirlooms like the kimonos Granny had brought from Japan, tea sets, lacquered tables, and one fine old set of china, blue and white porcelain, almost translucent. On the day we were leaving, Woody's car was so crammed with boxes and luggage and kids we had just run out of room. Mama had to sell this china.

One of the dealers offered her fifteen dollars for it. She said it was a full setting for twelve and worth at least two hundred. He said fifteen was his top price. Mama started to quiver. Her eyes blazed up at him. She had been packing all night and trying to calm down Granny, who didn't understand why we were moving again and what all the rush was about. Mama's nerves were shot, and now navy jeeps were patrolling the streets. She didn't say another word. She just glared at this man, all the rage and frustration channeled at him through her eyes.

He watched her for a moment and said he was sure he couldn't pay more than seventeen fifty for that china. She reached into the red velvet case, took a dinner plate and hurled it at the floor right in front of his feet.

The man leaped back shouting, "Hey! Hey, don't do that! Those are valuable dishes!"

Mama took out another dinner plate and hurled it at the floor, then another and another, never moving, never opening her mouth, just quivering and glaring at the retreating dealer, with tears streaming down her cheeks. He finally turned and scuttled out the door, heading for the next house. When he was gone, she stood there smashing cups and bowls and platters until the whole set lay in scattered blue and white fragments across the wooden floor.

---

3. **Samurai:** Japanese soldiers.

The American Friends Service helped us find a small house in Boyle Heights, another minority ghetto, in downtown Los Angeles, now inhabited briefly by a few hundred Terminal Island refugees. Executive Order 9066 had been signed by President Roosevelt, giving the War Department authority to define military areas in the western states and to exclude from them anyone who might threaten the war effort. There was a lot of talk about internment, or moving inland, or something like that in store for all Japanese Americans. I remember my brothers sitting around the table talking very intently about what we were going to do, how we would keep the family together. They had seen how quickly Papa was removed, and they knew now that he would not be back for quite a while. Just before leaving Terminal Island Mama had received her first letter, from Bismarck, North Dakota. He had been imprisoned at Fort Lincoln, in an all-male camp for enemy aliens.

Papa had been the patriarch.[4] He had always decided everything in the family. With him gone, my brothers, like councilors in the absence of a chief, worried about what should be done. The ironic thing is, there wasn't much left to decide. These were mainly days of quiet, desperate waiting for what seemed at the time to be inevitable.[5] There is a phrase the Japanese use in such situations, when something difficult must be endured. You would hear the older heads, the Issei, telling others very quietly, *"Shikata ga nai"* (It cannot be helped). *"Shikata ga nai"* (It must be done).

Mama and Woody went to work packing celery for a Japanese produce dealer. Kiyo and my sister May and I enrolled in the local school, and what sticks in my memory from those few weeks is the teacher—not her looks, her remoteness. In Ocean Park my teacher had been a kind, grandmotherly woman who used to sail with us in Papa's boat from time to time and who wept the day we had to leave. In Boyle Heights the teacher felt cold and distant. I was confused by all the moving and was having trouble with the classwork, but she would never help me out. She would have nothing to do with me.

This was the first time I had felt outright hostility from a Caucasian. Looking back, it is easy enough to

---

4. **patriarch:** male head of the family.
5. **inevitable:** unavoidable.

explain. Public attitudes toward the Japanese in California were shifting rapidly. In the first few months of the Pacific war, America was on the run. Tolerance had turned to distrust and irrational fear. The hundred-year-old tradition of anti-Orientalism on the west coast soon resurfaced, more vicious than ever. Its result became clear about a month later, when we were told to make our third and final move.

The name Manzanar meant nothing to us when we left Boyle Heights. We didn't know where it was or what it was. We went because the government ordered us to. And, in the case of my older brothers and sisters, we went with a certain amount of relief. They had all heard stories of Japanese homes being attacked, of beatings in the streets of California towns. They were as frightened of the Caucasians as Caucasians were of us. Moving, under what appeared to be government protection, to an area less directly threatened by the war seemed not such a bad idea at all. For some it actually sounded like a fine adventure.

Our pickup point was a Buddhist church in Los Angeles. It was very early, and misty, when we got there with our luggage. Mama had bought heavy coats for all of us. She grew up in eastern Washington and knew that anywhere inland in early April would be cold. I was proud of my new coat, and I remember sitting on a duffel bag trying to be friendly with the Greyhound driver. I smiled at him. He didn't smile back. He was befriending no one. Someone tied a numbered tag to my collar and to the duffel bag (each family was given a number, and that became our official designation[6] until the camps were closed), someone else passed out box lunches for the trip, and we climbed aboard.

I had never been outside Los Angeles County, never traveled more than ten miles from the coast, had never even ridden on a bus. I was full of excitement, the way any kid would be, and wanted to look out the window. But for the first few hours the shades were drawn. Around me other people played cards, read magazines, dozed, waiting. I settled back, waiting too, and finally fell asleep. The bus felt very secure to me. Almost half its passengers were immediate relatives. Mama and my older brothers had succeeded in keeping most of us together, on the same bus, headed for the same camp. I didn't realize until much later what a job that was. The strategy had been, first, to have everyone living in the same district when the evacuation began, and then to get all of us included under the same family number, even though names had been changed by marriage. Many families weren't as lucky as ours and suffered months of anguish while trying to arrange transfers from one camp to another.

We rode all day. By the time we reached our destination, the shades were up. It was late afternoon. The first thing I saw was a yellow swirl

---

6. **designation**: identification.

across a blurred, reddish setting sun. The bus was being pelted by what sounded like splattering rain. It wasn't rain. This was my first look at something I would soon know very well, a billowing flurry of dust and sand churned up by the wind through Owens Valley.

We drove past a barbed-wire fence, through a gate, and into an open space where trunks and sacks and packages had been dumped from the baggage trucks that drove out ahead of us. I could see a few tents set up, the first rows of black barracks, and beyond them, blurred by sand, rows of barracks that seemed to spread for miles across this plain. People were sitting on cartons or milling around, with their backs to the wind, waiting to see which friends or relatives might be on this bus. As we approached, they turned or stood up, and some moved toward us expectantly. But inside the bus no one stirred. No one waved or spoke. They just stared out the windows, ominously silent. I didn't understand this. Hadn't we finally arrived, our whole family intact? I opened a window, leaned out, and yelled happily. "Hey! This whole bus is full of Wakatsukis!"

Outside, the greeters smiled. Inside there was an explosion of laughter, hysterical, tension-breaking laughter that left my brothers choking and whacking each other across the shoulders.

We had pulled up just in time for dinner. The mess halls weren't completed yet. An outdoor chow line snaked around a half-finished building that broke a good part of the wind. They issued us army mess kits, the round metal kind that fold over, and plopped in scoops of canned Vienna sausage, canned string beans, steamed rice that had been cooked too long, and on top of the rice a serving of canned apricots. The Caucasian servers were thinking that the fruit poured over rice would make a good dessert. Among the Japanese, of course, rice is never eaten with sweet foods, only with salty or savory foods. Few of us could eat such a mixture. But at this point no one dared protest. It would have been impolite. I was horrified when I saw the apricot syrup seeping through my little mound of rice. I opened my mouth to complain. My mother jabbed me in the back to keep quiet. We moved on through the line and joined the others squatting in the lee of half-raised walls, dabbing courteously at what was, for almost everyone there, an inedible concoction.

After dinner we were taken to Block 16, a cluster of fifteen barracks that had just been finished a day or so earlier—although finished was hardly the word for it. The shacks were built of one thickness of pine planking covered with tarpaper. They sat on concrete footings, with about two feet of open space between the floorboards and the ground. Gaps showed between the planks, and as the weeks passed and the green wood dried out, the gaps widened. Knotholes gaped in the uncovered floor.

Each barracks was divided into six units, sixteen by twenty feet, about the size of a living room, with one bare bulb hanging from the ceiling and an oil stove for heat. We were assigned two of these for the twelve people in our family group; and our official family "number" was enlarged by three digits—16 plus the number of this barracks. We were issued steel army cots, two brown army blankets each, and some mattress covers, which my brothers stuffed with straw.

The first task was to divide up what space we had for sleeping. Bill and Woody contributed a blanket each and partitioned off the first room: one side for Bill and Tomi, one side for Woody and Chizu and their baby girl. Woody also got the stove, for heating formulas.

The people who had it hardest during the first few months were young couples like these, many of whom had married just before the evacuation began, in order not to be separated and sent to different camps. Our two rooms were crowded, but at least it was all in the family. My oldest sister and her husband were shoved into one of those sixteen-by-twenty-foot compartments with six people they had never seen before—two other couples, one recently married like themselves, the other with two teenage boys. Partitioning off a room like that wasn't easy. It was bitter cold when we arrived, and the wind did not abate. All they had to use for room dividers were those army blankets, two of which were barely enough to keep one person warm. They argued over whose blanket should be sacrificed and later argued about noise at night—the parents wanted their boys asleep by 9:00 p.m.—and they continued arguing over matters like that for six months, until my sister and her husband left to harvest sugar beets in Idaho. It was grueling work up there, and wages were pitiful, but when the call came through camp for workers to alleviate the wartime labor shortage, it sounded better than their life at Manzanar. They knew they'd have, if nothing else, a room, perhaps a cabin of their own.

That first night in Block 16, the rest of us squeezed into the second room— Granny, Lillian, age fourteen, Ray, thirteen, May, eleven, Kiyo, ten, Mama, and me. I didn't mind this at all at the time. Being youngest meant I got to sleep with Mama. And before we went to bed I had a great time jumping up and down on the mattress. The boys had stuffed so much straw into hers, we had to flatten it some so we wouldn't slide off. I slept with her every night after that until Papa came back.

Unit 4: Poetry

How do poems grow?
They grow out of your life.
                                        Robert Penn Warren

People often write about what they know best. As you read the poems in this unit, you will discover that many grew out of the poets' own experiences in life. The first two poems grew out of encounters with nature. The third deals with how people treat each other. The last poem expresses the frustration of seeing dreams constantly put off.

To understand how these poems grew, you will need to think about your own experiences. You have much to draw upon in your life. Relate what you already know to what you read. You will discover that with each reading, you will gain a deeper understanding of the poem.

While you read the poems, you may want to jot down your reactions. With each reading, a new thought may occur or a different feeling may surface. You will want to remember everything that the poem brings to mind. After reading each poem several times, look at your reactions. From these notes, you might be eager to write your own poem. Remember, you have experienced much in life, and from these experiences, poems grow!

What do you do to catch a moment's peace when you're very busy? In "Stopping by Woods on a Snowy Evening," the speaker takes time to watch snow falling in the quiet woods. What causes the speaker to leave this peaceful scene?

Stopping by Woods on a Snowy Evening

Robert Frost (1874–1963)

SILENT DAWN; Walter Launt Palmer; The Metropolitan Museum of Art, George A. Hearn Fund, 1921. (21.38)

Whose woods these are I think I know.
His house is in the village, though;
He will not see me stopping here
To watch his woods fill up with snow.

5 My little horse must think it queer
To stop without a farmhouse near
Between the woods and frozen lake
The darkest evening of the year.

He gives his harness bells a shake
10 To ask if there is some mistake.
The only other sound's the sweep
Of easy wind and downy flake.

The woods are lovely, dark, and deep.
But I have promises to keep,
15 And miles to go before I sleep,
And miles to go before I sleep.

Have you ever been so close to an animal that you could look into its eyes? In this poem, the speaker quietly observes a bird. What details show that the speaker is a careful observer?

A Bird came down the Walk

Emily Dickinson (1830–1886)

A Bird came down the Walk—
He did not know I saw—
He bit an Angleworm in halves
And ate the fellow, raw,

5 And then he drank a Dew
From a convenient Grass—
And then hopped sidewise to the Wall
To let a Beetle pass—

He glanced with rapid eyes
10 That hurried all around—
They looked like frightened Beads, I thought—
He stirred his Velvet Head

Like one in danger, Cautious,
I offered him a Crumb
15 And he unrolled his feathers
And rowed him softer home—

Than Oars divide the Ocean,
Too silver for a seam—
Or Butterflies, off Banks of Noon
20 Leap, plashless as they swim.

In this poem, the speaker states two ways to treat people who come from different ethnic backgrounds. Read to discover what the speaker feels is the best way. Do you agree with him?

From

The People, Yes

Carl Sandburg (1878–1967)

The copperfaces, the red men, handed us tobacco,
the weed for the pipe of friendship,
also the bah-tah-to, the potato, the spud.
Sunflowers came from Peruvians in ponchos.
5　Early Italians taught us of chestnuts,
walnuts and peaches being Persian mementos,
Siberians finding for us what rye might do,
Hindus coming through with the cucumber,
Egyptians giving us the onion, the pea,
10　Arabians handing advice with one gift:
"Some like it, some say it's just spinach."
　　To the Chinese we have given
　　　　kerosene, bullets, Bibles
and they have given us radishes, soy beans, silk,
15　poems, paintings, proverbs, porcelain, egg foo yong,
gunpowder, Fourth of July firecrackers, fireworks,
and labor gangs for the first Pacific railways.

PAINTED TEXTILE, 17th century (1630-1640) India, Golconda or Northern Madras. Painted plain
cloth weave; L: 275 W: 96 cm. The Brooklyn Museum, 14.7.19.6, Museum Collection Fund

Now we may thank these people
or reserve our thanks
20   and speak of them as outsiders
and imply the request,
"Would you just as soon get off the earth?"
holding ourselves aloof in pride of distinction
saying to ourselves this costs us nothing
25   as though hate has no cost
as though hate ever grew anything worth growing.
Yes we may say this trash is beneath our notice
or we may hold them in respect and affection
as fellow creepers on a commodious planet
30   saying, "Yes you too you too are people."

*What words do you use to describe your dreams? As you
read "Harlem," pay close attention to the words the
speaker uses. What do you think has happened to the
speaker's dreams to cause this outlook on life?*

Harlem

Langston Hughes (1902–1967)

What happens to a dream deferred?[1]

  Does it dry up
  like a raisin in the sun?
  Or fester like a sore—
5 And then run?
  Does it stink like rotten meat?
  Or crust and sugar over—
  like a syrupy sweet?

  Maybe it just sags
10 like a heavy load.

  Or does it explode?

---

1. deferred: put off; delayed.

Unit 5: Drama

All the world's a stage,
And all the men and women merely players...
Shakespeare

In this unit, you will read excerpts from two dramas. Like the short story and novel, the drama or play has characters, setting, and plot. But a play is meant to be presented by actors before an audience. You will want to approach your reading of a play with this in mind.

The written text of a play is called the script. The script of a play looks very different from other forms of literature. Notice that the names of the characters are followed by the words they say aloud. These words are called dialogue. Other words in italics and enclosed in parentheses are stage directions. These explain how the characters speak and act. Read these stage directions closely. They will help you understand what the characters are feeling and how their dialogue should be read. They will also help you picture the setting and the action.

After you read the excerpts from the plays, you and your classmates may be eager to read them aloud or perform them. You'll soon find that you are caught up in the highly charged experience that is drama!

The Younger family lives in a small apartment in Chicago. Mama, her son Walter, her daughter-in-law Ruth, and her grandson Travis share these cramped living quarters. For years the dreams of the family have seemed out of reach. A ray of hope is introduced when Mama receives $10,000 from her late husband's life insurance policy. But Mama and Walter disagree over what to do with the money.

As the scene opens, Walter and Ruth are talking about their family that seems to be falling apart. Mama comes home with a plan to pull the family together. As you read, consider how successful you think this plan will be.

A Raisin in the Sun

Lorraine Hansberry (1930–1965)

Ruth: Oh, Walter . . . *(Softly)* Honey, why can't you stop fighting me?
Walter: *(Without thinking)* Who's fighting you? Who even cares about you?
(This line begins the retardation of his mood)
Ruth: Well—*(She waits a long time, and then with resignation¹ starts to put away her things)* I guess I might as well go on to bed . . . *(More or less to herself)* I don't know where we lost it . . . but we have . . . *(Then, to him)* I—I'm sorry about this new baby, Walter. I guess maybe I better go on and do what I started . . . I guess I just didn't realize how bad things was with us . . . I guess I just didn't really realize—*(She starts out to the bedroom and stops)* You want some hot milk?
Walter: Hot milk?
Ruth: Yes—hot milk.
Walter: Why hot milk?
Ruth: 'Cause after all that liquor you come home with you ought to have something hot in your stomach.

---

1. **resignation:** patient acceptance.

Walter: I don't want no milk.

Ruth: You want some coffee then?

Walter: No, I don't want no coffee. I don't want nothing hot to drink. *(Almost plaintively)* Why you always trying to give me something to eat?

Ruth: *(Standing and looking at him helplessly)* What else can I give you, Walter Lee Younger?

(She stands and looks at him and presently turns to go out again. He lifts his head and watches her going away from him in a new mood which began to emerge when he asked her "Who cares about you?")

Walter: It's been rough, ain't it, baby? *(She hears and stops but does not turn around and he continues to her back)* I guess between two people there ain't never as much understood as folks generally thinks there is. I mean like between me and you—*(She turns to face him)* How we gets to the place where we scared to talk softness to each other. *(He waits, thinking hard himself)* Why you think it got to be like that? *(He is thoughtful, almost as a child would be)* Ruth, what is it gets into people ought to be close?

Ruth: I don't know, honey. I think about it a lot.

Walter: On account of you and me, you mean? The way things are with us. The way something done come down between us.

Ruth: There ain't so much between us, Walter...Not when you come to me and try to talk to me. Try to be with me...a little even.

Walter: *(Total honesty)* Sometimes... Sometimes...I don't even know how to try.

Ruth: Walter—

Walter: Yes?

Ruth: *(Coming to him, gently and with misgiving, but coming to him)* Honey... life don't have to be like this. I mean sometimes people can do things so that things are better...You remember how we used to talk when Travis was born...about the way we were going to live...the kind of house...*(She is stroking his head)* Well, it's all starting to slip away from us...

(Mama enters, and Walter jumps up and shouts at her)

Walter: Mama, where have you been?

Mama: My—them steps is longer than they used to be. Whew! *(She sits down and ignores him)* How you feeling this evening, Ruth?

(Ruth shrugs, disturbed some at having been prematurely interrupted and watching her husband knowingly)

Walter: Mama, where have you been all day?

Mama: *(Still ignoring him and leaning on the table and changing to more comfortable shoes)* Where's Travis?

Ruth: I let him go out earlier and he ain't come back yet. Boy, is he going to get it!

Walter: Mama!

Mama: *(As if she has heard him for the first time)* Yes, son?

Walter: Where did you go this afternoon?

Mama: I went downtown to tend to some business that I had to tend to.

Walter: What kind of business?

Mama: You know better than to question me like a child, Brother.

Walter: *(Rising and bending over the table)* Where were you, Mama?

(Bringing his fists down and shouting) Mama, you didn't go do something with that insurance money, something crazy?

(The front door opens slowly, interrupting him, and Travis peeks his head in, less than hopefully)

Travis: *(To his mother)* Mama, I—

Ruth: "Mama I" nothing! You're going to get it, boy! Get on in that bedroom and get yourself ready!

Travis: But I—

Mama: Why don't you all never let the child explain hisself.

Ruth: Keep out of it now, Lena.

(Mama clamps her lips together, and Ruth advances toward her son menacingly)

Ruth: A thousand times I have told you not to go off like that—

Mama: *(Holding out her arms to her grandson)* Well—at least let me tell him something. I want him to be the first one to hear...Come here, Travis. *(The boy obeys, gladly)* Travis—*(She takes him by the shoulder and looks into his face)*—you know that money we got in the mail this morning?

Travis: Yes'm—

Mama: Well—what do you think your grandmama gone and done with that money?

Travis: I don't know, Grandmama.

Mama: *(Putting her finger on his nose for emphasis)* She went out and she bought you a house! *(The explosion comes from Walter at the end of the revelation[2] and he jumps up and turns away from all of them in a fury. Mama continues, to Travis)* You glad about the house? It's going to be yours when you get to be a man.

Jacob Lawrence. TOMBSTONES. 1942. Gouache on paper. 28¾ x 20½ inches. Collection of Whitney Museum of American Art. Purchase. 43.14

Travis: Yeah—I always wanted to live in a house.

Mama: All right, gimme some sugar then—*(Travis puts his arms around her neck as she watches her son over the boy's shoulder. Then, to Travis, after the embrace)* Now when you say your prayers tonight, you thank God and your grandfather—'cause it was him who give you the house—in his way.

Ruth: *(Taking the boy from Mama and pushing him toward the bedroom)* Now you get out of here and get ready for your beating.

Travis: Aw, Mama—

---

2. **revelation:** piece of news.

Ruth: Get on in there—*(Closing the door behind him and turning radiantly to her mother-in-law)* So you went and did it!

Mama: *(Quietly, looking at her son with pain)* Yes, I did.

Ruth: *(Raising both arms classically)* Praise God! *(Looks at Walter a moment, who says nothing. She crosses rapidly to her husband)* Please, honey—let me be glad...you be glad too. (She has laid her hands on his shoulders, but he shakes himself free of her roughly, without turning to face her) Oh, Walter...a home...a home. (She comes back to Mama) Well—where is it? How big is it? How much it going to cost?

Mama: Well—

Ruth: When we moving?

Mama: *(Smiling at her)* First of the month.

Ruth: *(Throwing back her head with jubilance)* Praise God!

Mama: *(Tentatively, still looking at her son's back turned against her and Ruth)* It's—it's a nice house too... (She cannot help speaking directly to him. An imploring[3] quality in her voice, her manner, makes her almost like a girl now) Three bedrooms—nice big one for you and Ruth...Me and Beneatha still have to share our room, but Travis have one of his own—and *(With difficulty)* I figure if the—new baby—is a boy, we could get one of them double-decker outfits...And there's a yard with a little patch of dirt where I could maybe get to grow me a few flowers...And a nice big basement...

Ruth: Walter honey, be glad—

Mama: *(Still to his back, fingering things on the table)* 'Course I don't want to make it sound fancier than it is...It's just a plain little old house—but it's made good and solid—and it will be *ours*. Walter Lee—it makes a difference in a man when he can walk on floors that belong to *him*...

Ruth: Where is it?

Mama: *(Frightened at this telling)* Well—well—it's out there in Clybourne Park—

(Ruth's radiance fades abruptly, and Walter finally turns slowly to face his mother with incredulity and hostility)

Ruth: Where?

Mama: *(Matter-of-factly)* Four o six Clybourne Street, Clybourne Park.

Ruth: Clybourne Park? Mama, there ain't no colored people living in Clybourne Park.

Mama: *(Almost idiotically)* Well, I guess there's going to be some now.

Walter: *(Bitterly)* So that's the peace and comfort you went out and bought for us today!

Mama: *(Raising her eyes to meet his finally)* Son—I just tried to find the nicest place for the least amount of money for my family.

Ruth: *(Trying to recover from the shock)* Well—well—'course I ain't one never been 'fraid of no crackers, mind you—but—well, wasn't there no other houses nowhere?

Mama: Them houses they put up for colored in them areas way out all seem to cost twice as much as other houses. I did the best I could.

---

3. imploring: pleading.

Ruth: *(Struck senseless with the news, in its various degrees of goodness and trouble, she sits a moment, her fists propping her chin in thought, and then she starts to rise, bringing her fists down with vigor, the radiance spreading from cheek to cheek again)* Well—well!—All I can say is—if this is my time in life—*my time*—to say good-bye—*(And she builds with momentum⁴ as she starts to circle the room with an exuberant, almost tearfully happy release)*—to these Goddamned cracking walls!—*(She pounds the walls)*—and these marching roaches!—*(She wipes at an imaginary army of marching roaches)*—and this cramped little closet which ain't now or never was no kitchen!... then I say it loud and good, Hallelujah! and good-bye misery...I don't never want to see your ugly face again! *(She laughs joyously, having practically destroyed the apartment, and flings her arms up and lets them come down happily, slowly, reflectively, over her abdomen, aware for the first time perhaps that the life therein pulses with happiness and not despair)* Lena?

Mama: *(Moved, watching her happiness)* Yes, honey?

Ruth: *(Looking off)* Is there—is there a whole lot of sunlight?

Mama: *(Understanding)* Yes, child, there's a whole lot of sunlight.

(Long pause)

Ruth: *(Collecting herself and going to the door of the room Travis is in)* Well— I guess I better see 'bout Travis. *(To Mama)* Lord, I sure don't feel like whipping nobody today!

(She exits)

Mama: *(The mother and son are left alone now and the mother waits a long time, considering deeply, before she speaks)* Son—you—you understand what I done, don't you? *(Walter is silent and sullen⁵)* I—I just seen my family falling apart today...just falling to pieces in front of my eyes...We couldn't of gone on like we was today. We was going backwards 'stead of forwards—talking 'bout killing babies and wishing each other was dead . . . When it gets like that in life—you just got to do something different, push on and out and do something bigger... *(She waits)* I wish you say something, son...I wish you'd say how deep inside you you think I done the right thing—

Walter: *(Crossing slowly to his bedroom door and finally turning there and speaking measuredly)* What you need me to say you done right for? *You* the head of this family. You run our lives like you want to. It was your money and you did what you wanted with it. So what you need for me to say it was all right for? *(Bitterly, to hurt her as deeply as he knows is possible)* So you butchered up a dream of mine— you—who always talking 'bout your children's dreams...

Mama: Walter Lee—

(He just closes the door behind him. Mama sits alone, thinking heavily)

Curtain

---

4. momentum: speed.
5. sullen: moody.

I Remember Mama is a play about a Norwegian immigrant family living in San Francisco in the early 1900s. In the following scene, the oldest daughter Katrin recalls events that occur when her youngest sister Dagmar returns home from a long hospital stay. Other characters include Mama; Papa; a son Nels; the middle daughter Christine; Mama's sister Jenny; Mr. Hyde, a boarder in the home; and a soda clerk. As you read, think about who is the strongest member of the family.

From

I Remember Mama

John Van Druten (1901–1957)

Katrin: *(Reading)* "It wasn't very often that I could get Mama to talk—about herself, or her life in the old country, or what she felt about things. You had to catch her unawares, or when she had nothing to do, which was very, very seldom. I don't think I can ever remember seeing Mama unoccupied." *(Laying down the manuscript and looking out front.)* I do remember one occasion, though. It was the day before Dagmar came home from the hospital. And as we left, Mama suggested treating me to an ice-cream soda. *(She rises, gets her hat from beside her—a schoolgirl hat—puts it on and crosses while she speaks the next lines.)* She had never done such a thing before, and I remember how proud it made me feel—just to sit and talk to her quietly like a grown-up person. It was a kind of special *treat*-moment in my life that I'll always remember—quite apart from the soda, which was *wonderful. (Mama has come from between the curtains, and starts down the steps.)*

Mama: Katrin, you like we go next door, and I treat you to an ice-cream soda?

Katrin: *(Young now, and overcome)* Mama—do you mean it?

Mama: Sure. We celebrate. We celebrate that Dagmar is well, and coming home again. *(They cross to the turntable, which represents a drug-store, with a table and two chairs at which they seat themselves. Mama is at the left of the table.)* What you like to have, Katrin?

Katrin: *(With desperate earnestness)* I think a chocolate...no, a strawberry ...no, a chocolate soda.

Mama: *(Smiling)* You are sure?

Katrin: *(Gravely)* I think so. But, Mama, can we *afford* it?

Mama: I think this once we can afford it.

(The Soda Clerk appears.)

Soda Clerk: What's it going to be, ladies?

Mama: A chocolate ice-cream soda, please—and a cup of coffee.

(The Soda Clerk goes.)

Katrin: Mama, he called us "ladies"! *(Mama smiles.)* Why aren't you having a soda, too?

Mama: Better I like coffee.

Katrin: When can I drink coffee?

Mama: When you are grown up.

Katrin: When I'm eighteen?

Mama: Maybe before that.

Katrin: When I graduate?

Mama: Maybe. I don't know. Comes the day you are grown up, Papa and I will know.

Katrin: Is coffee really nicer than a soda?

Mama: When you are grown up, it is.

Katrin: Did you used to like sodas better...before you were grown up?

Mama: We didn't have sodas before I was grown up. It was in the old country.

Katrin: *(Incredulous)* You mean they don't have sodas in Norway?

Mama: Now, maybe. Now I think they have many things from America. But not when I was a little girl.

(The Soda Clerk brings the soda and the coffee.)

Soda Clerk: There you are folks. *(He sets them down and departs.)*

Katrin: *(After a good pull at the soda)* Mama, do you ever want to go back to the old country?

Mama: I like to go back once to look, maybe. To see the mountains and the fjords. I like to show them once to you all. When Dagmar is big, maybe we all go back once...one summer...like tourists. But that is how it would be. I would be tourist there now. There is no one I would know any more. And maybe we see the little house where Papa and I live when we first marry. And...*(Her eyes grow misty and reminiscent)* something else I would look at.

Katrin: What is that? *(Mama does not answer.)* What would you look at, Mama?

Mama: Katrin, you do not know you have brother? Besides Nels?

Katrin: No! A brother? In Norway? Mama...

Mama: He is my first baby. I am eighteen when he is born.

Katrin: Is he there now?

Mama: *(Simply)* He is dead.

Katrin: *(Disappointed)* Oh. I thought you meant...I thought you meant a real brother. A long-lost one, like in stories. When did he die?

Mama: When he is two years old. It is his grave I would like to see again. *(She is suddenly near tears, biting her lip and stirring her coffee violently, spilling some. She gets her handkerchief from her pocketbook, dabs at her skirt, then briefly at her nose, then she returns the handkerchief and turns to Katrin again. Matter-of-factly.)* Is good your ice-cream soda?

Katrin: *(More interested now in Mama than in it)* Yes. Mama...have you had a very *hard* life?

Mama: *(Surprised)* Hard? No. No life is easy all the time. It is not meant to be. *(She pours the spilled coffee back from the saucer into her cup.)*

Katrin: But...rich people...aren't *their* lives easy?

Mama: I don't know, Katrin. I have never known rich people. But I see them sometimes in stores and in the streets, and they do not *look* as if they were easy.

Katrin: Wouldn't you like to be rich?

Mama: I would like to be rich the way I would like to be ten feet high. Would be good for some things—bad for others.

Katrin: But didn't you come to America to *get* rich?

Mama: *(Shocked)* No. We come to America because they are all here—all the others. Is good for families to be together.

Katrin: And did you like it right away?

Mama: Right away. When we get off the ferry boat and I see San Francisco and all the family, I say: "Is like Norway," only it is better than Norway. And then you are all born here, and I become American citizen. But not to get rich.

Katrin: *I* want to be rich. Rich and famous. I'd buy you your warm coat. When are you going to get that coat, Mama?

Mama: Soon now, maybe—when we pay doctor, and Mr. Hyde pay his rent. I think now I *must* ask him. I ask him tomorrow, after Dagmar comes home.

Katrin: When I'm rich and famous, I'll buy you lovely clothes. White satin gowns with long trains to them. And jewelry. I'll buy you a pearl necklace.

Mama: We talk too much! *(She signs to the Soda Clerk.)* Come, finish your soda. We must go home. *(The Soda Clerk comes.)* How much it is, please?

Soda Clerk: Fifteen cents.

Mama: Here are two dimes. You keep the nickel. And thank you. Was good coffee. *(They start out and up the steps towards the curtains.)* Tomorrow Dagmar will be home again. And, Katrin, you see Uncle Elizabeth is there. This afternoon again she was asking for him. *(They disappear behind the curtains. After a second, the howls of a cat in pain are heard from behind the curtains—low at first, then rising to a heart-rending volume, and then diminishing again as the curtains part on the kitchen once more. Mama, Papa, and Dagmar are entering the house.)*

Dagmar: *(Standing on the threshold, transfixed)* It's Uncle Elizabeth, welcoming me home! That's his song of welcome. Where is he, Mama? *(She* *looks around for the source of the howls.)*

Mama: He is in the pantry...*(As Dagmar starts to rush thither.)* But wait...wait a minute, Dagmar. I must tell you. Uncle Elizabeth is...sick.

Dagmar: Sick? What's the matter with him?

Papa: He has been in a fight. Last night. He come home this morning very sick indeed.

(Dagmar starts for the pantry door, as Nels comes out.)

Mama: Nels, how is Uncle Elizabeth? Nels has been doctoring him.

Nels: He's pretty bad, Mama. I've dressed all his wounds again with boric acid, but...*(As Dagmar tries to get past him.)* I wouldn't go and see him now, baby.

Dagmar: I've got to. He's my cat. I haven't seen him in a whole month. More. *(She runs into the pantry and disappears.)*

Mama: Nels, what do you think?

Nels: I think we ought to have had him put away before she came home.

Mama: But she would have been so unhappy if he was not here *at all.*

Nels: She'll be unhappier still if he dies.

(Another howl is heard from the pantry, and then Dagmar comes rushing back.)

Dagmar: Mama, what happened to him? What happened to him? Oh, Mama...when I tried to pick him up, his bandage slipped over his eye. It was bleeding. Oh, Mama, it looked awful. Oh...*(She starts to cry.)*

Mama: *(Fondling her)* He looks like that all over. Nels, you go see to his eye

again. *(Wearily, Nels returns to the pantry.)* Listen, Dagmar...*Lille Ven*... would it not be better for the poor thing to go quietly to sleep?

Dagmar: You mean—go to sleep and never wake up again? *(Mama nods gently.)* No.

Papa: I think he die, anyway. Nels try to make him well. But I do not think he can.

Dagmar: Mama can. Mama can do everything. *(Another howl from offstage. She clutches Mama agonizedly.)* Make him live, Mama. Make him well again. *Please!*

Mama: We see. Let us see how he gets through the night. And now, Dagmar, you must go to bed. I bring you your supper.

Dagmar: But you will fix Uncle Elizabeth? You promise, Mama?

Mama: I promise I try. Go now. *(Dagmar goes out.)* I must fix her supper. *(She starts for the pantry. Howls again. She and Papa stand and look at each other. Nels comes out.)*

Nels: Mama, it's just cruelty, keeping that cat alive.

Mama: I know.

Papa: *(As another howl, the loudest yet, emerges)* You say we see how the cat get through the night. I ask you how do *we* get through the night? Is no use, Marta. We must put the cat to sleep. Nels, you go to the drugstore, and get something. Some chloroform,[1] maybe. *(He gives him a coin.)*

Nels: How much shall I get?

Papa: You ask the man. You tell him it is for a cat. He knows. *(Nels goes out*

---

1. **chloroform:** liquid used to stop pain or cause death.

and down the street. Looking at Mama's face.) Is best. Is the only thing.

Mama: I know. But poor Dagmar. It is sad homecoming for her. And she has been so good in hospital. Never once she cry. *(She pulls herself together.)* I get her supper. *(Another howl from off stage.)* And I take the cat outside. Right outside, where we...where *Dagmar* cannot hear him. *(She goes into the pantry. Papa takes a folded newspaper from his pocket, puts on his glasses and starts to read. The back door opens gently and Mr. Hyde peeps out. He wears his hat and coat and carries his suitcase and a letter. Papa has his back to him. Mr. Hyde lays the letter on the dresser and then starts to tiptoe across to the door. Then Papa sees him.)*

Papa: You go out, Mr. Hyde?

Mr. Hyde: *(Pretending surprise)* Oh...Oh, I did not see you, Mr. Hanson. *(He puts down the suitcase.)* I did not know you were back. As a matter of fact, I...I was about to leave this letter for you. *(He fetches it.)* The fact is...I...I have been called away.

Papa: So?

Mr. Hyde: A letter I received this morning necessitates my departure. My immediate departure.

Papa: I am sorry. *(Mama returns with a tray, on which are milk, bread, butter, and jelly.)* Mama, Mr. Hyde says he goes away.

Mama: *(Coming to the table with the tray)* Is true?

Mr. Hyde: Alas, dear madam, yes. 'Tis true, 'tis pity. And pity 'tis, 'tis true. You will find here...*(He presents the letter)* my check for all I owe you, and a note expressing my profoundest thanks for all your most kind hospitality. You will say good-by to the children for me? *(He bows, as Mama takes the letter.)*

Mama: *(Distressed)* Sure. Sure.

Mr. Hyde: *(Bowing again)* Madam, my deepest gratitude. *(He kisses her hand. Mama looks astonished. He bows to Papa.)* Sir—my sincerest admiration! *(He opens the street door.)* It has been a privilege. Ave atque vale! Hail and farewell! *(He makes a gesture and goes.)*

Mama: Was wonderful man! Is too bad. *(She opens the letter, takes out the check.)*

Papa: How much is check for?

Mama: Hundred ten dollar! Is four months.

Papa: Good. Good.

Mama: Is wonderful. Now we pay doctor everything.

Papa: And you buy your warm coat. With fur now, maybe.

Mama: *(Sadly)* But there will be no more reading. You take the check, Lars. You get the money?

Papa: *(Taking it)* Sure. I get it. What does he say in his letter?

Mama: You read it while I fix supper for Dagmar. *(She starts to butter the bread, and spread jelly, while Papa reads.)*

Papa: *(Reading)* "Dear Friends, I find myself compelled to take a somewhat hasty departure from this house of happiness..."

Mama: Is beautiful letter.

Papa: *(Continuing)* "I am leaving you my library for the children..."

Mama: He leaves his books?

Papa: He says so.

Mama: But is wonderful. Go see, Lars. See if they are in his room. *(Papa lays down the letter and goes out. Nels and Christine appear, coming up to the house. Christine carries schoolbooks.)*

Christine: I'm sure it was him, Nels. Carrying his suitcase, and getting on the cable car. I'm sure he's going away.

Nels: Well, I hope he's paid Mama. *(They open the street door.)*

Christine: *(Bursting in)* Mama, I saw Mr. Hyde getting on the cable car.

Mama: I know. He leave.

Christine: Did he pay you?

Mama: Sure, he pay me. Hundred ten dollar...

Nels: Gee...

Mama: *(Smiling)* Is good.

Christine: Are you going to put it in the Bank?

Mama: We need it right away. *(Papa returns, staggering under an armload of books.)* Mr. Hyde leaves his books, too. For you.

Nels: Say! *(Papa stacks them on the table. Nels and Christine rush to them, reading the titles.)* The Pickwick Papers, The Complete Shakespeare...

Christine: *Alice in Wonderland, The Oxford Book of Verse...*

Nels: *The Last of the Mohicans, Ivanhoe...*

Christine: We were right in the middle of that.

Mama: Nels can finish it. He can read to us now in the evenings. He has a fine voice, too, like Mr. Hyde. *(Nels flushes with pleasure.)* Is wonderful. So much we can learn. *(She finishes the supper-making.)* Christine, you take the butter back to the cooler for me, and the yelly, too. *(Christine does so.)* I go up to Dagmar now. *(She lifts the tray, then pauses.)* You get it, Nels?

Nels: What?...Oh...*(Taking a druggist's small bottle from his pocket.)* Here.

Mama: You put it down. After I come back, we do it. You know how?

Nels: Why, no, Mama, I...

Mama: You do not ask?

Nels: No, I...I thought Papa...

Mama: You know, Lars?

Papa: No, I don't *know*...but it cannot be difficult. If you *hold* the cat...

Mama: And watch him die? No! I think better you get rags...and a big sponge, to soak up the chloroform. You put it in the box with him, and cover him over. You get them ready out there.

Nels: Sure, Mama.

Mama: I bring some blankets.

(Nels goes off to the pantry, as Christine comes back. Again Mama lifts the tray and starts for the door. But there is a knock on the street door from Aunt Jenny, who has come to the house in a state of some excitement.)

Mama: *(Agitated)* So much goes on! See who it is, Christine.

Christine: *(Peeping)* It's Aunt Jenny. *(She opens the door.)*

Mama: Jenny...

Jenny: *(Breathless)* Marta...has he gone?

Mama: *(Above table)* Who?

Jenny: *(Near table)* Your boarder... Mr. Hyde...

Mama: Yes, he has gone. Why?

Jenny: Did he pay you?

Mama: Sure he pay me.

Jenny: How?

Mama: He give me a check. Lars has it right there.

Jenny: *(With meaning)* A check!

Mama: Jenny, what is it? Christine, you give Dagmar her supper. I come soon. *(Christine takes the tray from her and goes out.)* What is it, Jenny? How do you know that Mr. Hyde has gone?

Jenny: I was at Mr. Kruper's down the street...you know, the restaurant and bakery...and he told me Mr. Hyde was there today having his lunch, and when he left he asked if he would cash a check for him. For fifty dollars. *(She pauses.)*

Papa: Well, go on.

Jenny: Your fine Mr. Hyde didn't expect Mr. Kruper to take it to the bank until tomorrow, but he did. And what do you think? Mr. Hyde hasn't even an *account* at that bank! *(Nels returns and stands in the pantry doorway.)*

Mama: I don't understand.

Papa: *(Taking the check from his pocket)* You mean the check is no good?

Jenny: No good at all. *(Triumphantly.)* Your Mr. Hyde was a crook, just as I always thought he was, for all his reading and fine ways. Mr. Kruper said he'd been cashing them all over the neighborhood. *(Mama stands quite still, without answering.)* How much did he owe you? Plenty, I'll bet. *(Still no answer.)* Eh? Marta, I said I bet he owed you plenty. Didn't he?

Mama: *(Looks around, first at Nels and then down at the books on the table. She touches them)* No. No, he owed us nothing. *(She takes the check from Papa, tearing it.)* Nothing.

Jenny: *(Persistently)* How much was that check for? *(She reaches her hand for it.)*

Mama: *(Evading her)* It does not matter. He pay with better things than money. *(She goes to the stove, where she throws the check, watching it burn.)*

Jenny: I told you right in the beginning that you shouldn't trust him. But you were so sure...just like you always are. Mr. Hyde was a gentleman. A gentleman! I bet it must have been a hundred dollars that he rooked you of. Wasn't it?

Mama: *(Returning to the table)* Jenny, I cannot talk now. Maybe you don't have things to do. I have.

Jenny: *(Sneeringly)* What? What have *you* got to do that's so important?

Mama: *(Taking up the medicine bottle, fiercely)* I have to chloroform a cat! *(Jenny steps back in momentary alarm, almost as though Mama were referring to her, as she goes out into the pantry with the medicine bottle, not so very unlike Lady Macbeth with the daggers. Blackout and curtains close. After a moment, the curtains part again on the kitchen, the next morning. The books have been taken off the table, and Mama is setting the breakfast dishes, with Papa helping her. Dagmar comes bursting into the room.)*

Dagmar: Good morning, Mama. 'Morning, papa. Is Uncle Elizabeth all better?

Mama: Dagmar, there is something I must tell you.

Dagmar: I want to see Uncle Elizabeth first. *(She runs into the pantry. Mama turns helplessly to Papa.)*

Mama: Do something! Tell her!

Papa: If we just let her think the cat die . . . by itself . . .

Mama: No. We cannot tell her lies.

(Papa goes to the pantry door, opening it.)

Dagmar: *(Heard in pantry, off)* What a funny, funny smell. Good morning, my darling, my darling Elizabeth. *(Mama and Papa stand stricken. Dagmar comes in, carrying the cat, wrapped in an old shirt, with its head covered. She comes over to the table.)* My goodness, you put enough blankets on him! Did you think he'd catch cold?

Mama: *(Horror-stricken)* Dagmar, you must not . . . *(She stops at the sight of the cat, whose tail is twitching, quite obviously alive.)* Dagmar, let me see . . . Let me see the cat! *(She goes over to her, below the table front, and uncovers the cat's head.)*

Dagmar: *(Overjoyed)* He's well. Oh, Mama, I *knew* you'd fix him.

Mama: *(Appalled)* But, Dagmar, I didn't, I . . .

Dagmar: *(Ignoring her)* I'm going to take him right up and show him to Nels. *(She runs off, calling.)* Nels! Nels! Uncle Elizabeth's well again!

Mama: *(Turning to Papa)* Is a miracle! *(She sits, dumfounded, on the bench in front of the table.)*

Papa: *(Beside her, shrugging)* You cannot have used enough chloroform. You just give him good sleep, and that cures him. We rechristen the cat, Lazarus![2]

Mama: But, Lars, we must tell her. Is not *good* to let her grow up believing I can fix *everything!*

Papa: Is best thing in the world for her to believe. *(He chuckles.)* Besides, I know *exactly* how she feels. *(He lays his hand on hers.)*

Mama: *(Turning with embarrassment from his demonstrativeness and slapping his hand)* We finish getting breakfast. *(She turns back to the table.)*

---

2. **Lazarus:** a man raised from the dead by Jesus.